The Art of War
Interpreted for Real Estate Investors

Strategic Thinking for Acquiring Property, Beating Competition, and Winning Deals

ANCIENT WISDOM HACKS

Publisher: NX Inc

Third Edition

Contents

Preface

Why a 2,500-Year-Old War Manual Still Rules Modern Markets

Property markets may look like spreadsheets and deeds, but under the hood they run on conflict—buyers versus sellers, debt versus equity, optimism versus risk. Sun Tzu saw the pattern long before cap rates and zoning boards:

> "All warfare is based on deception." — *The Art of War*, I

Deals swing on imperfect information—off-market whispers, cosmetic staging, massaged rent rolls. Your edge comes from seeing the hidden shape of the board faster than the other side.

> "Victorious warriors win first and then go to war." — IV

Underwriting is that pre-battle victory: you stress-test costs, lock funding, model exits, and only then write an offer. Walk into escrow half-prepared and you're the general scrambling on the field.

> "In the midst of chaos, there is also opportunity." — II

Rising rates, policy shocks, neighborhood upheaval—chaos scares tourists out of the market and hands disciplined operators first pick of the spoils.

Author's Real-Estate War Stories: Wins, Blunders, Rescues

Win — The 28-Unit Sneak Attack

A bank-owned apartment sat on the market 180 days. Everyone assumed the boilers were toast. Quiet due-diligence revealed a $6 fuse, not a $60 k replacement. I closed at a 9.7 % cap; twelve months later a REIT bought at a 6 %.

> Lesson: "He who is prudent and lies in wait for an enemy who is not, will be victorious." — III

Blunder — The Overleveraged Flip

I believed my own pro-forma, ignored contingency budgets, and chased price momentum. Contractor delays bled my hard-money clock dry; I exited breakeven after fees.

> Lesson: "If you know neither the enemy nor yourself, you will succumb in every battle." — III

Rescue — The Fire-Damaged Fourplex

Inherited mid-renovation chaos from a burnt-out seller. I stabilized insurance, structured a seller carry, moved tenants to temp housing, rebuilt in 90 days, and refinanced all cash out.

Lesson: "The skillful soldier does not raise a second levy." — III

These scars and trophies are woven into every chapter so you can copy the wins and dodge the land mines.

Promise to You, the Reader

This book is a field manual, not a coffee-table prop. By the last page you will be able to:

1. **Sharpen Strategy** – Map each Sun Tzu principle to concrete deal moves: sourcing, funding, rehab, exit.

2. **Strip Emotion** – Replace gut reactions with checklists, stop-loss triggers, and "pre-mortem" drills.

3. **Boost ROI** – Capture upside others miss and defend downside others accept.

"Opportunities multiply as they are seized." — V

Treat every worksheet, case study, and drill as live ammo. Work through them, refine them, run them again. Master the art, and the market—chaotic or calm—will start to look less like a battlefield and more like open, navigable ground.

Chapter 1

Know Yourself, Know the Market

> "If you know the enemy and know yourself, you need
> not fear the result of a hundred battles."
> —*Sun Tzu, The Art of War*, ch. 3

A century of real-estate deals lives or dies on that single sentence. Sun Tzu pours twenty-five characters of ancient Chinese into a timeless principle: edge comes from clarity—clarity about what *you* bring to the field and what the *market* is likely to throw back. This chapter drills that principle into a practical operating system for investors. We will map your internal landscape—capital, risk tolerance, deal velocity—and then overlay it on the external landscape—cycles, local micro-markets, competitor behavior. When both maps line up, entries look obvious, exits feel natural, and surprises shrink to annoyances instead of disasters.

---

1. Why Self-Knowledge Beats Raw Capital

Sun Tzu never wrote about cap rates, but he understood capital's fatal flaw: money without strategy invites ruin.

> "He will win who, prepared himself, waits to take the
> enemy unprepared."
> —ch. 10

Most new investors focus on the spreadsheet, skip the mirror, and end up chasing deals that look good on social media but don't fit their balance sheet or lifestyle. You cannot outsource self-knowledge to a mentor or underwriter; you must build it brick by brick. That starts with a brutally honest Investor SWOT.

2. The Investor SWOT

SWOT stands for Strengths, Weaknesses, Opportunities, Threats. We'll narrow the lens to three variables that dominate every residential or commercial investment you will ever sign:

1. **Capital** — cash, credit lines, partner equity, and borrowing power.

2. **Risk Tolerance** — the emotional and financial pain you can absorb without freezing.

3. **Deal Velocity** — how fast your personal machine can source, close, stabilize, and recycle capital.

2.1 Capital

Cash is a strategic weapon, but only when you understand its range and reload time. Sun Tzu reminds us:

> "In war, numbers alone confer no advantage."
> —ch. 9

A $5 million balance sheet with every dollar tied up in slow refi queues can be weaker than a $200 k stash of liquid hard-money commitments. Your *capital profile* breaks down into:

- **Dry Powder**: money you can wire within seventy-two hours.

- **Committed Reserves**: capital already earmarked for rehabs, reserves, or partner distributions.

- **Expandable Lines**: HELOCs, business credit cards, partnership capital calls.

- **Unreliable Hopes**: potential raises, verbal JV promises, speculative refi proceeds.

If you mislabel hopes as dry powder you will walk into escrow unprepared and pay for someone else's timetable.

2.2 Risk Tolerance

Risk tolerance is not attitude; it is capacity. It wraps your mental bandwidth, household budget, and career stability into a single variable. Sun Tzu again:

> "The general who loses his head in the heat of battle
> is unfit to command."
> —ch. 8

Measure risk tolerance like a thermostat, not a slogan. Track:

- **Monthly Carry Maximum**: the dollar amount you can float in vacancies or cost overruns before selling personal assets.

- **Sleep Disruption Line**: the threshold—often lower—where anxiety sabotages decision-making.

- **Replenishment Rate**: how fast employment income or operating cash flow rebuilds reserves after a drawdown.

Real estate loves to test every one of those numbers at the same time.

2.3 Deal Velocity

Deal velocity is your turnover rate: offers written per month, contracts accepted per quarter, closings per year, and refis or exits per cycle. It includes the tempo of your team—brokers, lenders, contractors—and the friction of your market's bureaucracy.

> "Speed is the essence of war."
> —ch. 11

High velocity is not inherently superior. A surgeon and a field medic both save lives, but they train for different cadences. Match your velocity to your capital cycle and stress ceiling; otherwise you will sprint into a wall.

3. Knowing the Market

Self-knowledge without market intelligence is a monk meditating on a cliff. You need *both*. Sun Tzu devotes multiple chapters to terrain, weather, and enemy disposition. Translate those into:

- **Macro Cycles**: interest rates, employment trends, legislative changes, demographic shifts.

- **Micro Terrain**: neighborhood rent curves, school-zone rezoning, transit-line extensions, flood-zone revisions.

- **Competitor Presence**: institutional buyers, flipper saturation, out-of-state capital chasing yield compression.

> "He who knows the terrain and the enemy has won
> half the battle."
> —paraphrase of ch. 10

Spend fifteen minutes on the Federal Reserve's FRED database, and the edge begins. Spend three hours interviewing local property managers, and comps start telling secrets. Spend three weeks walking blocks at dawn and again at midnight, and sub-markets reveal whether your underwriting stress tests are generous or naïve.

---

4. Building the Personal Balance-Sheet War Room

The War Room is a living dashboard—part notebook, part database, part alarm system. It keeps the "know yourself" side updated in real time, then angles that knowledge against live market feeds. Set it up once, refine it forever.

Action Checklist

1. **Inventory the Arsenal**

   o Pull last month's bank, brokerage, and credit-line statements.

   o Mark liquid versus locked funds.

   o Assign every dollar to Dry Powder, Committed Reserves, Expandable Lines, or Unreliable Hopes.

2. **Plot the Emotional Perimeter**

   o Journal your worst-case vacancy loss and rehab overrun scenarios.

   o Log physiological responses: heart rate spike, insomnia, distraction.

   o Set a Sleep Disruption Line number—the loss amount where symptoms ignite.

3. **Draft the Velocity Grid**

   o Audit your calendar: hours per week available for sourcing, due diligence, and asset management.

- Log turnaround times for lenders, inspectors, and contractors.

  - Commit to a target cadence (e.g., "one offer every two weeks, one close per quarter").

4. **Install Early-Warning Sensors**

  - Subscribe to three macro-cycle newsletters (e.g., Fed rate updates, local chamber of commerce bulletins, housing starts reports).

  - Set Google Alerts for your top two ZIP codes plus keywords like "rezoning," "tax levy," "crime spike."

  - Schedule quarterly lunch with a title officer—they see distress before the MLS does.

5. **Run the First Stress Drill**

  - Choose a hypothetical 20 % rent drop and a 2 % interest-rate bump.

  - Model the effect on each asset and on your consolidated cash flow.

  - Identify which property or partnership fails first; plan contingencies: rate caps, rental concessions, asset sales.

6. **Codify Decision Gates**

   o Green Zone: parameters within capital reserves
     and sleep comfort—execute.

   o Yellow Zone: parameters strain reserves 25
     %—pause, require second approval.

   o Red Zone: breaches sleep line—abort or exit per
     pre-written plan.

7. **Publish and Rehearse**

   o Print a one-page dashboard; tape it to your office
     monitor.

   o Review with spouse, partner, or accountability
     group monthly.

   o After each closed deal, conduct a five-minute
     debrief: did the War Room predict the friction, or did
     reality surprise you?

"What enables the wise sovereign and the good
general to strike and conquer, and achieve things
beyond the reach of ordinary men, is foreknowledge."
—ch. 13

Foreknowledge is not mystic foresight; it is structured awareness.

5. From Insight to Tactics: Practical Crossovers

Knowing yourself and the market is only valuable when it shows up in tomorrow morning's task list. Below are concrete swivel-points where your War Room outputs direct tactical choices.

5.1 Offer Strategy

If Dry Powder is slim but Expandable Lines are deep, offer longer close, bigger earnest money, and inspection waivers backed by bridge finance. If Dry Powder is fat and velocity targets are high, write low-ball offers with twenty-four-hour closings; some sellers will trade price for certainty.

5.2 Financing Mix

High Risk Tolerance and fast Velocity? Hard money and novation contracts may fit. Moderate Risk Tolerance? Blend conventional 30-year debt with private money seconds. Low Risk Tolerance? Stick to stabilized multi-family under agency debt; accept lower IRR for sleep and scale.

5.3 Asset Class Selection

Heavy capital but low emotional bandwidth? Triple-net retail or self-storage automation beats dumpster fires behind D-class apartments. Limited capital but high hunger for chaos? Deep value-add multifamily or brownfield redevelopment may suit.

> "Do not repeat the tactics which have gained you one victory, but let your methods be regulated by the

infinite variety of circumstances."
—ch. 6

Your War Room prevents copy-and-paste investing. It drives bespoke moves tuned to present resources and terrain.

---

6. Case Interlude: Two Investors, Two Outcomes

Investor A—No War Room
 Jumps into a six-unit with full-price offer because "rents are low; just raise them." Underestimated tenant resistance, vacancy hits 50 %, private lender calls note early, forced sale at loss. Post-mortem shows zero Dry Powder and risk blind spots.

Investor B—War Room Discipline
 Spots same property, but War Room flags capital shortfall and low sleep line. Passes. Three months later picks up a fourplex from a divorce sale at 80 % of market. War Room stress test already drilled a 25 % vacancy scenario; performance exceeds plan, cash-out refi in sixteen months.

Outcome difference is not luck. Investor B knew self, knew market, struck where probability was bent in his favor.

---

7. Common Pitfalls and How to Counter Them

1. **Overconfidence in Expandable Lines**
   Counter: require written, date-stamped commitments

before counting partner equity.

2. **Lagging KPI Updates**
   Counter: automate data pulls to a spreadsheet and block fifteen-minute Friday review slot.

3. **Ignoring the Sleep Disruption Line**
   Counter: spouse or partner veto if proposed deal moves reserves within 10 % of the line.

4. **Mismatched Velocity**
   Counter: quarterly review—if actual velocity exceeds target by 50 % or more, halt new sourcing until crew, capital, and systems grow.

"There are roads which must not be followed, armies which must not be attacked, towns which must not be besieged."
—ch. 8

Rejecting a shiny deal can be a bigger win than closing a mediocre one.

---

8. Iterating the War Room

The War Room is not a corkboard snapshot; it is a living commander's hut. Schedule these upgrades:

- **Quarterly**: refresh FICO scores, equity appraisals, and debt-service coverage ratios.

- **Semi-Annual**: revise risk tolerance after any major life change—marriage, job loss, new child.

- **Annual**: audit velocity logs; prune low-return funnels (e.g., wholesaler lists with sub-5 % hit rate).

After every full market cycle—roughly five to eight years—tear the dashboard down and rebuild from scratch. The general who won yesterday may be obsolete tomorrow.

---

9. Mindset Calibration

Sun Tzu's thesis is ultimately psychological. He trains generals to remove ego and emotion long enough to see truth. The War Room is your anti-ego device.

> "Appear weak when you are strong, and strong when you are weak."
> —ch. 1

When the spreadsheet glows green, ask the War Room to find hidden red. When fear whispers, let the War Room show hard numbers that fear is lying.

Greed and anxiety run the same con: they hijack attention. Your structured dashboards, stress drills, and decision gates keep attention anchored to reality. Every quarter you push numbers through the model is one more quarter you train emotional neutrality.

---

10. Next Steps

By the end of this chapter you should have:

- A documented Investor SWOT broken into capital, risk tolerance, and velocity.

- A Personal Balance-Sheet War Room with live data feeds and tripwires.

- A first stress drill completed and weaknesses exposed.

Carry that intel forward. Chapter 2 expands the scope from personal balance sheets to Sun Tzu's Five Factors—Mission, Cycle, Location, Team, Process—so that your War Room plugs seamlessly into campaign-level strategy. Over time the two systems merge; you evolve from combatant to commander.

> "Opportunities multiply as they are seized."
> —ch. 5

Seize the first: know yourself, know the market. Everything else in this book—and every deal you ever ink—builds on that foundation.

Chapter 2

The Five Factors

> "The art of war is governed by five constant factors, to
> be taken into account in one's deliberations, when
> seeking to determine the conditions obtaining in the
> field."
> —*Sun Tzu, The Art of War*, ch. 1

Sun Tzu opens his treatise with a checklist. Before scouts march, before swords leave scabbards, a commander stacks five lenses against reality and refuses to flinch until the picture snaps into focus. Miss even one of the lenses, and the picture blurs; the campaign dissolves into luck.

Modern real-estate investors fight with spreadsheets instead of spears, yet the five factors remain fatal or fantastic depending on your discipline. This chapter digs into each, translates them into the language of property and capital, and builds a weekly ritual—thirty minutes, no excuses—that keeps the lenses clean.

---

1. Translating the Five Factors

Sun Tzu's original list reads: **Moral Law, Heaven, Earth, the Commander, Method and Discipline.** We will recast them as **Mission, Cycle, Location, Team, Process**—five anchors you can tape to an office wall, build into slide decks, and annotate after every investment committee meeting.

1. **Moral Law → Mission**

2. **Heaven → Cycle**

3. **Earth → Location**

4. **Commander → Team**

5. **Method → Process**

Each pair is more than wordplay; it is a calibrated bridge from bronze-age warfare to twenty-first-century asset management.

1.1 Moral Law → Mission

> "The Moral Law causes the people to be in complete accord with their ruler, so that they will follow him regardless of their lives, undismayed by any danger."
> —ch. 1

In real estate, Moral Law is the *why* that rallies money, contractors, tenants, regulators, and neighbors into alignment. Swap "people" for "stakeholders." Without that north-star clarity, teams drift, lenders hedge, and communities block permits.

Your **Mission** answers three questions in a single sentence:

- **Outcome** – What value will this portfolio create?

- **Stakeholder Benefit** – Who wins besides you?

- **Time Horizon** – When will success be obvious?

Example: *"Acquire and reposition Class C multifamily in working-class transit corridors to provide clean, affordable housing and deliver an annualized 15 % IRR to partners within five years."*

The sentence is short because war rooms forget long manifestos. Speak it at every kickoff meeting until the mission is muscle memory.

1.2 Heaven → Cycle

> "Heaven signifies night and day, cold and heat, times
> and seasons."
> —ch. 1

Heaven is everything cosmic you cannot bend but must anticipate: weather, climate, tides. For investors, **Cycle** captures macro currents—interest-rate regimes, credit availability, demographic bulges, policy tides.

Markets punish ignorance of Heaven. Buy floating-rate debt at the top of a tightening cycle, and rising LIBOR will gut cash flow faster than any leaky roof. Buy during an expansion with a recession-proof capital stack, and you look prophetic.

1.3 Earth → Location

> "Earth comprises distances, great and small; danger
> and security; open ground and narrow passes; the
> chances of life and death."
> —ch. 1

Location is the immortal real-estate cliché, but Sun Tzu widens the frame: not just *where*, but *how the ground behaves under stress*. Distance to job centers, floodlines, gentrification spillovers, infrastructure upgrades—all shape risk and upside.

Location forces you to diagram micro-terrain:

- commute patterns today versus ten-year transport plans,

- school-district boundaries scheduled for redraw,

- zoning overlays one council vote away from change.

Ignore Earth, and you mis-price hazard or miss upside baked into the soil.

1.4 Commander → Team

> "The Commander stands for the virtues of wisdom,
> sincerity, benevolence, courage, and strictness."
> —ch. 1

Deals do not fail for lack of models; they fail for lack of humans you can trust when models melt. **Team** means sponsor, property manager, GC, attorney, broker, leasing staff—every hand that touches the asset.

Sun Tzu's five virtues translate cleanly:

- **Wisdom** – competence, skill stacking, pattern recognition.

- **Sincerity** – transparent reporting, no hidden fees.

- **Benevolence** – caring about tenant outcomes and partner liquidity.

- **Courage** – willingness to take contrarian positions backed by data.

- **Strictness** – enforcing standards even when uncomfortable.

A single missing virtue corrodes the rest; the portfolio absorbs the cost.

1.5 Method → Process

> "By Method and Discipline are to be understood the marshaling of the army in its proper subdivisions, the graduations of rank, the maintenance of roads by which supplies may reach the army, and the control of

military expenditure."
—ch. 1

Process is every repeatable checklist, SOP, system, and tool that turns chaos into throughput—Kanban boards, construction draw checklists, asset-management scorecards, monthly investor letters. Method puts velocity on rails; discipline keeps the rails straight.

---

2. Deep Dive: Mapping Macro Cycles to "Heaven"

Sun Tzu did not command the weather; he studied cloud patterns, counted harvest moons, calculated march pace against monsoon season, and attacked when Heaven tilted odds. Real-estate operators must do the same.

2.1 The Four Macro Dimensions

1. **Cost of Capital** – Interest-rate trajectories, yield-curve shape, lender risk appetite.

2. **Liquidity Flows** – Institutional allocations, securitization gates, regional-bank health.

3. **Policy Climate** – Tax incentives, rent controls, zoning rewrites, environmental regulations.

4. **Demographic Momentum** – Population growth, migration corridors, household formation.

Each dimension oscillates; combine the oscillations and you get a market weather report.

2.1.1 Cost of Capital

Rising rates compress values; falling rates inflate cap rates if NOI keeps pace. But nuance matters: a flattening yield curve signals recession odds; a steepening curve can follow aggressive stimulus. Track both headline rate and spread to the ten-year Treasury.

> "He who can modify his tactics in relation to his opponent and thereby succeed in winning, may be called a heaven-born captain."
> —ch. 6

A heaven-born investor locks long-term, fixed-rate debt when spreads are thin and cushions adjustable exposure with interest-rate caps before volatility spikes.

2.1.2 Liquidity Flows

If pension funds crank allocations to real-estate debt, bridge-loan supply spikes and underwriting loosens. That invites over-leverage hazards eighteen months later. Conversely, a bank panic freezes construction lending; shovel-ready projects stall, supply pipeline shrinks, and stabilized owners enjoy rent pressure.

Liquidity trends often precede price moves; watch fund-raising announcements, CMBS issuance, and bank loan-deposit ratios.

2.1.3 Policy Climate

Municipalities wobble between NIMBY and YIMBY; federal tax codes oscillate between acceleration and clawback. A single state-level rent-control bill can disintegrate pro-forma assumptions overnight. Likewise, a new Opportunity Zone classification can inject equity floodwaters into a previously overlooked district.

Track proposed legislation—not just passed bills—and map partisan composition of committees; probabilities surface months before headlines.

2.1.4 Demographic Momentum

Census data, driver's-license change-of-address files, school-enrollment figures—they chart demand before brokers notice. Millennials aging into family formation spike suburbs; retirees chasing sunbelt health care glut senior-living demand.

Heaven's demographic stars shift slowly but relentlessly; ignoring them causes vacancy surges that no granite countertop can cure.

2.2 Building the Heaven Dashboard

1. **Interest-Rate Gauge** – Track Fed Funds upper band, SOFR, ten-year Treasury, and AAA CMBS spread.

2. **Liquidity Index** – Aggregate CMBS issuance, REIT net-acquisition stats, regional bank CRE loan growth.

3. **Policy Heatmap** – Maintain spreadsheet of pending housing bills with status, committee stage, and probability score.

4. **Demographic Ticker** – Quarterly update of county-level population change, job growth, and median wage trend.

Each metric alone hints; together they forecast.

---

3. Toolbox: The 30-Minute Macro Tracker

Five factors preach insight, not homework paralysis. The question: how to stay current without devouring your week? Below is a time-boxed routine—thirty minutes once a week—that keeps you five steps ahead of passive buyers.

3.1 Preparation

- **Calendar Block** – Same half-hour every Friday morning before inbox screams.

- **Single Dashboard File** – One spreadsheet or Notion board with five tabs (Mission, Cycle, Location, Team, Process).

- **Auto-Feeds** – RSS or email feeds delivering macro data snapshots to a folder: Fed releases, state legislature trackers, Census updates.

The ritual survives only if friction is near zero.

3.2 Minute-by-Minute Breakdown

1. **Minutes 1-3: Mission Pulse**

   - Re-read mission sentence aloud.

   - Ask: Does news this week challenge the premise? Example: new rent cap bill may contradict "deliver 15 % IRR." Note to revisit underwriting if yes.

2. **Minutes 4-12: Cycle Scan**

   - Open rate spreadsheet. Update latest Fed Funds, SOFR, ten-year Treasury yields. Note direction: ↑,

↓, or ↔.

- Glance at CMBS issuance data point emailed by Trepp or similar.

- Skim top two housing-policy headlines sourced from saved Google Alert. Record them as potential (P) or enacted (E).

- Flag anomalies: sudden spike in CMBS spreads, or new statewide eviction moratorium.

3. **Minutes 13-18: Location Intel**

- Check local county building-permit stats via automatic feed. Rising permits signal supply surge.

- Scroll saved alerts for your key ZIP codes: crime blotter upticks, school district vote outcomes.

- Add bullet: "Subway extension funding approved—timeline 2028" to Location tab.

4. **Minutes 19-23: Team Review**

- Scan email threads from PM, GC, lender. Any evidence of virtue drift—missed report, budget overage, late draw?

- Jot one-sentence score next to each key member: Green, Yellow, or Red. Adverse trend triggers phone call.

5. **Minutes 24-28: Process Audit**

   - Pick one SOP checklist each week and ask: "Did we skip a step?" For instance, draw-request photo log.

   - If yes, append corrective action in Process tab: "Add photo timestamp requirement by Monday."

6. **Minutes 29-30: Commit**

   - Schedule follow-ups flagged above.

   - Save dashboard snapshot. Type single-line journal entry: "Week 27—Cycle stable, location news positive, team yellow (GC)."

Thirty minutes ends. Close dashboard. Weekend begins.

3.3 Why the Tracker Works

- **Compression** – Hard deadline forces prioritization; noise dies.

- **Iteration** – Weekly snapshots accumulate into trendlines; direction outranks single datapoints.

- **Integration** – Five tabs mirror five factors; mind links cause and effect organically.

> "The enlightened ruler lays his plans well ahead; the good general cultivates his resources."
> —ch. 2

The macro tracker is cultivation in calendar form.

---

4. Interlocking the Five Factors in Practice

The factors are not silos; they interlock like gears. A mission misaligned with demographic cycle drags location strategy, which strains team morale and exposes process cracks. A policy swing inside Heaven may mutate location risk overnight, forcing mission rewrite. Discipline is in tracing ripples.

4.1 Real-World Scenario: Rate-Shock Repricing

Heaven: The central bank jolts rates 150 bps in three meetings. *Cycle Tab registers red arrows.*

Location: Class A downtown rents flatten; suburban garden-style remains buoyant.
Team: Debt broker warns bridge lenders retreating.
Process: Acquisition checklist still assumes LTV 75 %.

Action Flow

1. Mission lens: delivering affordable housing looks safer than luxury reposition.

2. Cycle shift triggers underwrite at 65 % LTV fixed debt.

3. Location pivot: focus on suburbs inside 25-minute commute belt.

4. Team adaptation: add agency lender to capital stack roster.

5. Process amendment: revise LOI template with longer due diligence to secure rate lock.

Each factor cues adjustments downstream until portfolio posture realigns with reality.

4.2 Avoiding Factor Myopia

Sun Tzu warns against commanders who obsess over terrain while ignoring morale—or who trust to valour while starving supplies. In property terms: an investor hypnotized by demographic growth can overlook policy hostility; a spreadsheet ninja can discount team culture and sabotage execution. Weekly cross-factor review inoculates against such tunnel vision.

---

5. Building Organizational Memory Around the Five Factors

Rigor scales when shared. Embed the factors into company culture:

- **Onboarding** – First-day slide deck walks newbies through Mission, Cycle, Location, Team, Process.

- **Deal Memos** – Each section of investment memo labeled with corresponding factor; underwriters must justify assumption alignment.

- **Post-Mortems** – After exit, autopsy success or failure along five-factor axis: Which lens mis-read? What data missing?

> "If you know the enemy and know yourself, you need
> not fear the result of a hundred battles."
> —ch. 3

Expand "enemy" to macro forces, micro rivals, and operational entropy; know them in five dimensions.

---

6. Common Misinterpretations and How to Correct Them

1. **Moral Law as Marketing Feel-Good**
   Reality: Mission influences capital cost and political

goodwill—quantifiable.
Fix: Attach KPI—e.g., tenant satisfaction score, unit-turn cost—so mission impact shows up on P&L.

2. **Heaven as Unpredictable**
Reality: Nobody predicts rates perfectly, but tracking direction changes defensive posture from reaction to preemption.
Fix: Use probabilistic scenarios—base, bear, bull—and premortem each.

3. **Earth as GPS Coordinates Only**
Reality: Microterrain includes social fabric and future infrastructure.
Fix: Visit planning-commission meetings quarterly; fuse boots-on-ground with GIS layers.

4. **Commander as Single Person**
Reality: Even a solo GP leans on lender committees, property managers, partnership votes.
Fix: Map influence network; grade each node on virtue metrics.

5. **Method as SOP Binders Nobody Reads**
Reality: Process breathes only when tied to incentives and reviewed.
Fix: Gamify compliance—scorecards with bonuses for zero-defect draws or on-time unit turnovers.

Misinterpretations are costly not for their presence but for their invisibility. Shining five-factor light reveals them early.

7. From Factors to Advantage: Case Study in Application

Background: Mid-sized sponsor aims to enter a secondary market offering tax credits for workforce housing conversions.

Mission – Provide 20 % below-market rents while delivering 13 % IRR to investors over seven years.
Cycle – Fed tightening; state legislators expanding affordable-housing grants; migration inflow from coastal metros.
Location – Former textile warehouses walking distance to new light-rail spur.
Team – Sponsor partners with non-profit specialist in tax-credit compliance, local GC adept at adaptive reuse.
Process – Weekly cross-functional scrum; cloud dashboard tracking grant milestones; GC milestone-based draws.

Outcome: Completed 180-unit conversion under budget, stabilized at 97 % occupancy in twelve months, awarded additional credits for solar retrofit. Investors receive first distribution quarter early.

Every victory traceable to factor alignment: Heaven tailwind in policy, Earth selection near transit, Commander alliance sharing virtues, Method drilled weekly.

8. Continual Evolution: When Factors Drift

No plan survives contact with time. Mission may mature; Heaven flips regimes; Team turns over. Build "Factor Drift" checks:

- **Annual Mission Review** – Does original sentence still capture stakeholder reality?

- **Quarterly Heaven Reforecast** – Update base/bear/bull scenarios; rehearse liquidity crunch drill.

- **Semi-Annual Earth Recon** – Rent walks, traffic counts, drone surveys track gentrification or decay.

- **Bi-Monthly Team Feedback** – 360-degree reviews map virtue erosion early.

- **Process Kaizen Sessions** – Every forty-five days pick a checklist, cut steps, automate tasks.

Drift unchecked becomes gap; gap widens into breach; breach invites defeat.

---

9. Closing Thought

> "Therefore, in your deliberations, when seeking to determine the military conditions, let them be made the basis of a comparison, in this wise:—"
> —ch. 1

Sun Tzu ends the five-factor passage by urging comparison. Not just sensing conditions, but measuring them against each other: which general obeys Moral Law? Which army embraces discipline? Which terrain favors defense? Victory belongs to the side that tallies factors soberly and acts before the adversary notices.

Your adversary is not simply another buyer; it is mediocrity, inertia, and the blind spot of complacency. Weaponize Mission, Cycle, Location, Team, and Process; track Heaven in thirty minutes weekly; let the five factors click into place like gears. When they hum in unison, you need not fear the result of a hundred bids, a hundred site walks, a hundred capital calls. You will have earned the label Sun Tzu reserved for rare commanders: **invincible, because you made defeat impossible long before the battle began.**

Chapter 3

Victory Without Battle: Due Diligence as Espionage

"To fight and conquer in all your battles is not supreme
excellence; supreme excellence consists in breaking
the enemy's resistance **without** fighting."
—*Sun Tzu, The Art of War*, ch. 3

Real-estate investors rarely swing hammers or shout across
trenches, yet every accepted offer is a skirmish and every closing
a campaign. The seller's asking price, the broker's marketing
packet, even the glossy rent roll are camouflaged positions meant
to steer you into paying more, closing faster, and waiving
contingencies. Your counter-move is intelligence: you uncover,
verify, and pressure-test facts until the negotiated price contains
no surprises and the contract's risk is already neutralized. Sun Tzu
called this art **spy-craft**; modern operators call it **due
diligence**—the discipline of winning your profit before a single rent
check clears.

This chapter weaponizes three ideas:

1. **Gathering intel** beyond the brochure—county records,
   zoning boards, water-table maps, code-enforcement logs,
   and every off-balance-sheet whisper you can legally
   obtain.

2. **Red-teaming your own numbers** so ruthlessly that any
   flaw a savvy seller could exploit is exposed and corrected

by you first.

3. **Running a 48-hour micro-market recon drill** that turns raw data into ground truth, compressing months of learning into one weekend.

Walk through these pages as if you were training to infiltrate an adversary's headquarters. Because in high-stakes real estate, that's precisely what you are doing—only the adversary is opacity and the headquarters is a file drawer in a county clerk's office.

---

1 Why Due Diligence Equals Espionage

"All warfare is based on deception."
—ch. 1

The listing memorandum is a curated illusion: best-case rent increases, cherry-picked expense comps, photos snapped the hour after the landscapers left and the minute before rush-hour traffic snarled the street. Assume every unverified statement is an intentional or accidental distortion. Your mission: pierce illusions **before** contract deadlines force concessions.

- **Information asymmetry** favors the seller by default. They know the roof leaks twice a year, the HVAC is past half-life, and the tenant in unit 3B is a professional rent escaper.

- **Legal doctrine** in most states is "caveat emptor"—buyer beware. Unless fraud is provable, undisclosed defects become your burden after closing.

- **Capital markets** punish naivety. Undiscovered CapEx bombs or down-zoning threats vaporize debt-service coverage ratios overnight, and lenders have no pity for an operator who "didn't know."

Thus, you adopt the posture of a spy. You dig quietly, triangulate sources, and verify each fact twice. You win **without** litigation, renegotiation, or write-downs because you anticipated every angle.

---

2 Intelligence Channels: Where to Find the Unsaid

Sun Tzu employed five classes of spies; you will deploy five streams of intel. Each targets a gap in the glossy brochure and fills it with verifiable data.

2.1 County Records—the Paper Battlefield

> "The enlightened ruler lays his plans well ahead; the good general cultivates his resources."
> —ch. 2

At the county courthouse or, increasingly, on its website lies a timeline of every deed, lien, foreclosure notice, and tax delinquency. These public documents answer questions sellers gloss over:

- **Chain of Title** – Has the parcel bounced through shell entities? Multiple transfers in quick succession often flag distress or legal gymnastics.

- **Tax Arrears** – Outstanding balances imply cash-flow strain; a motivated lien settlement can shave thousands off purchase price.

- **Lis Pendens** – Pending lawsuits tell you whether a neighbor disputes easements or the property is entangled in probate.

Pulling the docket takes minutes and costs pennies; failing to pull it can cost the deal.

2.2 Zoning Boards—the Peace or the Minefield

Zoning governs what *can* exist, not what *does*. A small-town planner's file cabinet may hide conditional-use permits vital to your business plan—think short-term rentals, density bonuses, or food-truck pads. Conversely, a pending **down-zone**—from multifamily to single-family, for instance—can strangle a value-add strategy in its crib.

Attend one planning-and-zoning meeting in person. Listening to grievances about parking and height restrictions yields intelligence no online agenda captures: the board's political mood, the local activists' leverage, and whether your future variance request will glide or crash.

2.3 Water-Table and Environmental Maps—the Invisible Risk

Floods, soil contamination, and perched water tables ruin more pro formas than recessions. FEMA flood-zone overlays, state environmental databases, and USGS groundwater level charts are free. Study them. Layer your parcel on GIS maps to see:

- **100-Year Flood Lines** – Lenders may require pricey insurance, tenants demand move-in discounts, or FEMA may ban basements.

- **Brownfield Sites** – Proximity flags potential cleanup liens, vapor-intrusion testing, or endless Phase II studies.

- **High Water Tables** – Predict foundation heave, sewer backup, and hidden sump-pump expenses.

> "He who knows the terrain and the enemy has won
> half the battle."
> —ch. 10

Terrain today includes hydrology and hydrocarbon plumes.

2.4 Code-Enforcement and Permitting Logs—the Quiet Alarms

A city's code-enforcement office retains complaints: mold, pests, illegal wiring. A pattern of citations signals systemic issues—tenant quality, deferred maintenance, landlord attitude. Permitting logs show whether the HVAC replacement the seller touts actually passed inspection or whether it never happened.

Request reports under Freedom of Information statutes if needed. Government clerks rarely bite; a polite phone call and a coffee gift card go far.

2.5 Local Knowledge Networks

Brokers, property-management companies, and corner-store owners know truths the data misses: which block floods first, which tenant base threatens evictions, which landlord is off-loading properties because a massive assessment looms.

Cultivate relationships. Information flows to the investor who listens more than talks, buys lunch more than sells hype.

---

3 Red-Team Your Numbers Before the Seller Does

> "If you know the enemy and know yourself, you need
> not fear the result of a hundred battles."
> —ch. 3

Red-teaming is the discipline of attacking your own assumptions as viciously as an adversary would. You build the model on Monday; on Tuesday you put on a different hat and attempt to destroy it.

3.1 Target the Rent Roll

- **Verify Occupancy** – Call utilities or inspect meters to confirm units are truly occupied, not staged with a friend's furniture.

- **Lease Audits** – Cross-check sample leases against ledger; look for concessions absent from the rent column—free parking, cable packages, or deferred first month.

- **Seasonality Stress** – Model worst-case renewal months stacking in winter, when vacancy carries longer.

If 90 % occupancy drops to 82 % under scrutiny, your debt-coverage ratio may collapse.

3.2   Deconstruct the T-12

- **CapEx Masquerading as OpEx** – A one-time $30 k roof patch buried in "repairs" should be capitalized forward in your reserve budget.

- **Management Fees** – Are they below market because the owner self-managed? Adjust upward.

- **Real Estate Taxes** – Assessed value often resets at sale. Call the county assessor; derive the *post-sale* tax bill.

3.3   Validate Market Comps

> "What the ancients called a clever fighter is one who not only wins, but excels in winning with ease."
> —ch. 4

Ease is an illusion if your rent comps are cherry-picked. Visit competitor units, talk to leasing agents, verify advertised concessions. Scrape online listings to capture averaged asking rent, then discount by typical concession value. Build a worst-case rent matrix: if new supply delivers 300 units next quarter, where does your property sit?

3.4 Crew Cut Your Pro Forma

Slash projected rent growth to zero. Inflate insurance by 25 %. Add six months to your rehab timeline. Does the project survive? If not, you are paying for hope.

---

4 The 48-Hour Micro-Market Recon Drill

> "He who wishes to fight must first count the cost."
> —ch. 13

Counting cost means seeing with your own eyes. Two days on the ground compress weeks of remote guesswork. Below is a field manual.

4.1 Pre-Mission Briefing (Evening Before Day 1)

- Print maps: parcel, surrounding one-mile radius, transit lines.

- Load dashboards with county crime data, demographic trends, and pending development filings.

- List five competitor properties to visit.

- Book motel **inside** the neighborhood; you are living in the battlefield.

4.2   Day 1 Morning—Dawn Patrol

6:00 a.m.—Drive perimeter streets. Note potholes, traffic density, early-bird business activity. Observe tenant demographics leaving for work. Bad traffic flows or boarded storefronts foreshadow leasing challenges.

7:30 a.m.—Walk the subject property's alleyways and parking lots. Look for leaking dumpsters, graffiti under fresh paint, and makeshift cable runs—tells of deferred maintenance.

4.3   Day 1 Midday—Official Channels

10:00 a.m.—Drop in at city planning department unannounced. Review file drawings. Ask about upcoming transport or utility projects. Planners love to talk to interested citizens.

11:30 a.m.—Pull lunch at the closest diner. Chat with staff: "How's rent lately? Anyone moving out?" Locals voice truths brochure copywriters omit.

4.4   Day 1 Afternoon—Competitor Sweep

1:00 p.m.—Tour the five comps. Pose as tenant, collect pricing sheets, ask about concessions. Photograph lobby condition, parking rules, amenity usage. These become calibration points for your rent forecast.

3:30 p.m.—Meet property-management prospects. Gauge professionalism, staffing ratios, and response rates. Your team eval begins now.

4.5   Day 1 Evening—Night Vision

8:00 p.m.—Return to subject block. Streetlights reveal how safe tenants will feel. Measure decibel levels from adjacent bars or highways. Note license plates—local or transient?

10:00 p.m.—Drive a two-mile loop. Map police presence, loitering hotspots, and late-night traffic. The vibe at night often diverges sharply from daytime brochures.

4.6   Day 2 Morning—Systems Check

8:00 a.m.—Meet building engineer or inspector on-site. Open electrical panels, crawl attics, photograph serial numbers on mechanicals. Cross-reference with seller's CapEx list.

10:30 a.m.—Visit county recorder's office in person. Sometimes data not online sits in a drawer: old easement maps, unresolved liens.

4.7   Day 2 Midday—Stakeholder Interviews

12:00 p.m.—Lunch with local banker or broker. Ask pointed questions: What debt deals died recently? Any headlines coming? People share more over salad than Zoom.

1:30 p.m.—Knock on three tenant doors politely. Offer gift cards for five-minute surveys. Ask: How quick are repairs? Any planned rent hikes? Tenants love candor and expose managerial gaps.

4.8   Day 2 Late Afternoon—Synthesis

3:00 p.m.—Retreat to motel. Dump photos, audio notes, and brochures into one folder. Draft a one-page recon memo:

- Strengths – e.g., solid masonry, under-market rents verified.

- Weaknesses – e.g., water infiltration in boiler room, crime spike Friday nights.

- Opportunities – e.g., zoning allows 20 % more density, neighboring employer expanding.

- Threats – e.g., rival Class-B rehab 0.4 miles away with aggressive concessions.

5:00 p.m.—Send memo to partners before you leave town. Real-time intel spurs faster go/no-go decisions.

---

5   Case Study: The Condo Conversion That Never Closed

Investor duo found a 1920s four-story building marketed for condo conversion: "Historic charm! Zoning already approved!" They scheduled diligence but skipped courthouse liens and night patrol. Our firm audited for them 72 hours pre-closing.

- **County records** showed an unresolved mechanics lien from a previous HVAC contractor—$120 k plus 8 %

interest.

- **Zoning minutes** revealed neighbors appealing the variance on parking. Hearing date set two weeks after planned close.

- **Night recon** caught a freight line 200 yards away blasting horns at 2 a.m.—hidden by daytime brochure photos.

- **Water-table map** placed basement two feet below seasonal flood mark; flood insurance quote tripled budget.

They walked. The seller re-listed at a deep discount; disclosure of defects now mandatory. The due-diligence cost: $2 k. The avoided disaster: seven-figure.

> "The general who wins a battle makes many calculations in his temple ere the battle is fought."
> —ch. 1

Your "temple" is diligence; the saved capital is victory before first contact.

---

6 Common Espionage Pitfalls and How to Counter

1. **Data Overload Paralysis**
   Counter: Time-box research; seek decision-grade data, not perfection.

2. **Vendor Blind Spots**
    Counter. Hire two inspectors: one generalist, one
    specialist (roof, sewer, or environmental depending on
    asset).

3. **Confirmation Bias**
    Counter. Assign a teammate "Chief Skeptic." Their job is
    to disprove the deal.

4. **Relationship Complacency**
    Counter. Even trusted brokers have incentives; verify
    every claim through independent channels.

5. **Deadline Compression**
    Counter. Negotiating longer inspection periods beats
    rushing. Walk away if pushed to waive.

> "He will win who, prepared himself, waits to take the
> enemy unprepared."
> —ch. 10

Prepared means pitfalls neutralized before signatures dry.

---

7   Embedding an Espionage Culture

Due diligence becomes instinct when baked into company DNA:

- **Checklists** – Every asset class gets a living checklist. Add
  new failure modes after each post-mortem.

- **War-Games** – Quarterly drills: choose a held asset, imagine you are the plaintiff lawyer, regulator, or whistle-blower. What flaw could sink you? Patch it.

- **Reward Skepticism** – Celebrate team members who halt a deal for red flags; bonuses tied to *money saved*, not just incurred.

- **Debrief Rituals** – After each aborted contract, hold a no-fault debrief: what intel surfaced late? How to surface it earlier next time?

Culture ensures that espionage is not heroics but habit.

---

8 Conclusion: Profit Wears Camouflage

> "In the midst of chaos, there is also opportunity."
> —ch. 2

Chaos is the swirling haze around every transaction: compressed timelines, misaligned incentives, incomplete disclosures. Opportunity hides where others assume too much. Your espionage grade due-diligence pierces haze, extracts pattern, and positions you to either renegotiate or withdraw with minimal sunk cost.

Victory without battle is not metaphorical. It is withdrawing earnest money after discovering a buried oil tank the day before contingencies expire; it is renegotiating $200 k off purchase price after zoning minutes reveal inevitable parking assessments; it is securing lender comfort and investor confidence because your diligence binder leaves no page unturned. Every dollar preserved is yield earned; every disaster dodged is IRR boosted before cap-rate compression or rent growth even enter the equation.

Deploy the intel channels. Red-team until the spreadsheet bleeds. Run the 48-hour recon drill until neighborhood secrets feel like open files. Do these, and you will embody Sun Tzu's maxim: **"The greatest victory is that which requires no battle."**

Chapter 4

Position: Buy on Your Terms

> "Supreme excellence consists of breaking the
> enemy's resistance **without fighting**."
> —*Sun Tzu, The Art of War*, ch. 3

A perfect purchase is silent. No shouting matches, no protracted bidding wars, no twenty-third-hour rush to beat a higher offer. You secure the deed while your rival buyers are still sharpening pencils. That is Sun Tzu's "supreme excellence," and in real estate it hinges on **position**—the set of informational, psychological, and financial advantages you accumulate *before* you ever put ink to contract.

This chapter translates position into three leverage engines—**seller finance, option contracts, and partner splits**—then arms you with a **nine-question script vault** that surfaces a seller's private motivations so you can assemble terms they accept gladly. You will learn to win the property on your specifications, your timeline, and your downside protection while the seller feels heard, helped, and satisfied. Victory without violence, profit without combat.

---

1   The Philosophy of Position

> "He who can modify his tactics in relation to his
> opponent and thereby succeed in winning, may be

called a heaven-born captain."
—ch. 6

Most investors treat an offer as a static PDF: price, earnest money, inspection days. If that PDF is the same template everyone else uses, you have ceded initiative. Position begins earlier:

1. **Information Advantage** – private knowledge of the seller's pain points, lender constraints, and property idiosyncrasies.

2. **Term Flexibility** – multiple financing arrows in your quiver so you can swap structures mid-negotiation without scrambling for approvals.

3. **Speed of Execution** – the operational capacity to move from handshake to closing faster than the seller's anxiety clock.

Combine those three and resistance evaporates; the seller concedes not because you out-talked them, but because you removed every obstacle to the outcome they secretly desire.

---

2 Understanding the Seller's Battlefield

"If you know the enemy and know yourself, you need not fear the result of a hundred battles."
—ch. 3

"Enemy" here means *friction*, not villain. Every seller faces one or more frictions:

- **Payment Timing** – cash today versus income over years.

- **Tax Exposure** – capital-gains cliff that a straight sale would trigger.

- **Debt Trap** – balloon notes, adjustable-rate resets, or violation of loan covenants.

- **Management Burnout** – four a.m. plumbing calls that have killed their enthusiasm.

- **Family Dynamics** – heirs disagree, divorce settlement looms, probate drags.

- **Reputation Risk** – fear the neighborhood will learn the building has issues.

Your reconnaissance script will unearth which frictions dominate. Once identified, you can remove them with one of three core structures.

---

3 Offer Structure #1: Seller Finance

"When you surround an army, leave an outlet free."
—ch. 7

A seller note is that outlet: the owner exits active management but still enjoys interest income, amortization, and sometimes collateral protection superior to the stock market. You gain control with little or no bank underwriting and often at below-market rates.

3.1 Anatomy of a Seller Note

- **Purchase Price** – fixed or stepped.

- **Down Payment** – 5 %-20 % is common; some deals zero down if collateral strong.

- **Interest Rate** – negotiated; lower than hard money, higher than bank CDs.

- **Amortization** – interest-only, 30-year, or graduated payments.

- **Balloon** – five-year typical, aligned to your value-add timeline.

- **Security Instrument** – mortgage, deed of trust, or land contract depending on state.

3.2 Why Sellers Say Yes

- Defers or spreads capital-gains tax.

- Generates passive annuity replacing burnt-out landlord income.

- Beats bank CD yield with first-position collateral they already understand.

- Salvages deals when conventional financing denied due to property condition.

3.3 Investor Edge

- Lower closing costs—no origination, junk fees, or appraisal if negotiated.

- Flexible repayment schedule that mirrors stabilization curve.

- Speed—deal moves at the pace of two signatures, not underwriters.

---

4 Offer Structure #2: Option Contracts

> "To secure ourselves against defeat lies in our own hands."
> —ch. 4

An **option**—whether a straight purchase option, a lease-option, or an option wrapped in a master lease—secures control today, ownership tomorrow, at a strike price you choose now. It is the art of tying up opportunity while limiting downside.

4.1   Types of Options

1. **Straight Purchase Option** – Right, not obligation, to buy by a date at fixed price.

2. **Lease-Option** – Tenant-buyer leases property, a portion of rent credits against purchase.

3. **Master Lease with Option** – Investor controls income, operations, upside while deferring title transfer.

4.2   Why Sellers Say Yes

- Immediate relief from management without full sale.

- Maintains depreciation benefits until option exercised.

- Bridges seasoning period to clear liens or probate.

- "Test-drive" of buyer competence; seller sees payments before surrendering deed.

4.3   Investor Edge

- Low capital outlay—option fee instead of down payment.

- Time to arrange perm financing, entitlements, or rent lifts.

- Walk-away clause: if macro climate sours, option lapses, capital at risk is capped.

5 Offer Structure #3: Partner Splits

> "Thus the highest form of generalship is to balk the
> enemy's plans."
> —ch. 3

Sometimes the *enemy* is the seller's own fear of regret.
Joint-venture or equity-split agreements let them ride future upside
rather than exit entirely. You supply expertise, operations, and
sometimes capital; they supply property and possibly financing.

5.1 Models of Splits

- **Equity Swap** – Seller deeds property into new LLC;
  receives, say, 70 % equity, you 30 % for managing.

- **Preferred Return + Promote** – Investors earn fixed pref;
  after hurdle, profits split 50/50 or 70/30 to sponsor.

- **Hybrid** – Seller holds note plus minority equity, hedging
  income and upside.

5.2 Why Sellers Say Yes

- Emotional attachment to asset preserved via partial stake.

- Participate in future appreciation, especially if market
  heating.

- Defer entire tax event through contribution to entity under §721 (UPREIT) or §1031 co-tenancy transition.

- Offload headaches while maintaining identity as owner in community.

5.3 Investor Edge

- Little cash at close—your sweat equity valued.

- Aligned incentives—seller becomes ally in variance hearings or tenant relations.

- Access to legacy knowledge about building quirks, contractor history.

---

6 Combining Structures: Creative Hybrids

A deal is not limited to one play. Option can merge into seller finance on exercise. Seller finance can pair with equity earn-out if NOI surpasses hurdle. Example:

Year 0: Master lease with option for $50 k premium; you run rehab, boost NOI.

Year 2: Exercise option, seller carries 75 % of price at 4 % interest.

Year 5: Refinance repays seller, who retains 10 % equity kicker until resale.

Every clause addresses a specific pain or desire uncovered by your script vault.

---

7   Script Vault: Nine Questions to Flush Out Hidden Seller Pain

> "In war, then, let your great object be victory, not
> lengthy campaigns."
> —ch. 2

Lengthy negotiations waste goodwill. The following nine questions, delivered with genuine curiosity, expose motivators fast. Use them in order; each primes the next.

1. **"What's prompting you to sell now rather than hold another year?"**
   Isolate timing trigger—debt, health, partnership split.

2. **"How would an ideal sale feel for you on closing day?"**
   Surfaces emotional metrics—speed, simplicity, legacy.

3. **"Are there any ongoing payments or debts tied to the property you'd like to be free of?"**
   Probes debt traps you can assume or restructure.

4. **"If price weren't the only factor, what else would make this a win for you?"**
   Invites non-price levers—tax relief, continued cash flow, tenancy protection.

5. **"How do you feel about receiving income over time versus one lump sum?"**
   Opens door to seller finance or equity stake.

6. **"What concerns keep you up at night about the selling process?"**
   Draws out risk perceptions—appraisal, inspection delays, family objections.

7. **"Have you explored alternatives like refinancing, partnering, or partial sales?"**
   Gauges sophistication, positions you as advisor.

8. **"Is there a deadline on your side—for taxes, relocation, debt maturity—I should be aware of?"**
   Locks sun-set timeline that dictates structure length.

9. **"If we could craft a solution that solves the issues you've described, would you be open to a creative approach?"**
   Soft commitment; if yes, you have permission to propose seller note, option, or split.

Deliver these questions conversationally, not as interrogation. Between each, **listen**. Silence often reveals more than words; hesitation marks pain you can relieve.

8 From Intel to Term Sheet: A Five-Step Flow

1. **Discovery Call** – Deploy nine questions; take handwritten notes (signals seriousness).

2. **Rapid Synthesis** – Map each pain point to structure: tax → installment sale, burnout → master lease, debt maturity → quick close seller note.

3. **Term-Sheet Draft** – One-page bullet format outlining price, structure, timeline, contingencies. No legalese yet.

4. **Feedback Loop** – Present draft within 24 hours; ask seller to edit. Their redlines teach you final objections.

5. **Contract Execution** – Escrow attorney or title drafts formal docs aligned to chosen structure; you stay quarterback.

Speed demonstrates competence; customization earns trust.

---

9 Handling Pushback Without Breaking Rapport

"When the enemy shows an opening, be swift as a hare."
—ch. 7

If the seller balks:

- **Rate Too Low?** Offer interest-only period then step-up rate year three.

- **Option Fee Too Small?** Add non-refundable advance rent credit.

- **Equity Give-Up Feels High?** Counter with buyout clause at future appraisal multiple.

- **Family Worried About Security?** Assign deed of trust or personal guarantee.

Always trade concessions, never volunteer them. Each adjustment should correspond to a benefit for you: longer term, lower down, exclusive due diligence. Momentum matters more than purity.

---

10   Ethical Negotiation: Creating Value, Not Exploiting Pain

Sun Tzu advocates cunning but not cruelty. Creative terms should alleviate the seller's stress *and* secure your upside. If you weaponize knowledge to trick rather than serve, reputation capital shrinks, and deals sourced through referrals evaporate.

Guidelines:

- Disclose what the seller must know—funding capacity, timeline reality.

- Encourage third-party review—CPAs, attorneys.

- Leave goodwill residue—moving assistance, tenant care pledges, or public acknowledgment.

> "Build your opponent a golden bridge to retreat across."
> —ch. 7

The golden bridge is dignity and fair value.

---

11   Common Creative-Finance Pitfalls and Countermeasures

- **Usury and Dodd-Frank Limits** – Some states cap interest on seller notes; owner-occupied deals trigger consumer-credit rules. *Consult counsel.*

- **Due-On-Sale Clauses** – Wrap mortgages silently? Risk bank acceleration. Negotiate SNDA or formal assumption.

- **Title Seasoning** – Future refis may balk at quick value jumps; use appraiser packages documenting improvements.

- **Partnership Governance** – Outline decision rights, capital calls, exit procedures in operating agreement; ambiguity births litigation.

- **Option Recordation** – Unrecorded options can be ignored by new liens; record memorandum to secure rights.

Supreme excellence is risk neutralized prior to execution.

---

12   Case Snapshot: The Burnt-Out Landlord and the Ballooning Note

Scenario: 20-unit building, owner-operator aging out. Three months from a $450 k balloon payment his bank refuses to modify. Market price $1.8 M. Deferred maintenance scaring conventional buyers.

Applied Script: Questions #1, #2, #3 revealed primary pain: looming default and zero appetite for another rehab. Question #5 uncovered openness to income stream; taxes worried him.

Term Sheet:

- $1.8 M price.

- $90 k option fee, six-month term.

- Master lease at $10 k/month triple-net; NOI currently $8 k → you eat $2 k shortfall while renovating five vacancies.

- Purchase on or before month six for $1.62 M (option fee credit). Seller carries $1.3 M first-position note at 4 % interest-only five years; you bring $320 k private equity.

- Seller note payments $4.3 k/month—less than his old mortgage—solves cash need; balloon eliminated.

- You raise rents and refinance year three at $2.4 M valuation; pay off seller, pocket $700 k cash-out, retain asset stabilized at 8.5 % cash-on-cash.

No bidding war, no bank gatekeeping. Resistance broken before it formed.

---

13 Conclusion: The Art of the Invisible Win

"Hence to fight and conquer in all your battles is not supreme excellence; supreme excellence consists in breaking the enemy's resistance without fighting."
—ch. 3

Buying on your terms means the seller believes those terms are their idea or, at worst, their best refuge. Harness seller finance to soothe tax fears, deploy options to grant breathing room, craft partner splits to honor sentimental attachment, and wield your nine-question script to coax unspoken truths into daylight.

Position is not brute force; it is gravitational pull. When you master it, sellers orbit your solution set naturally. Deals close quietly, referrals flow freely, and you march on to the next campaign without ever firing a shot.

Chapter 5

Momentum: Funding the Campaign

> "The line between disorder and order lies in logistics."
> —*Sun Tzu, The Art of War*, ch. 2 [1]

Momentum in real-estate investing is not found in glossy brochures, viral marketing, or even a killer off-market pipeline. Momentum is cash that arrives on time, in the right tranche, and in the right account—*every single day of the holding period*. Lose that flow for even a quarter and the whole campaign shudders; lose it for a year and it bleeds out on the balance sheet.

Sun Tzu did not talk about cap-ex draws or interest-only bridge notes, but he did obsess over grain, war chests, and wagon trains. He knew that without a protected supply line—money, food, materiel—no army survives long enough to deploy its superior strategy. In property terms, your capital stack *is* the supply line. Guard it before you guard the roof, the tenants, even the brand. This chapter shows how.

1   Capital Stack ≡ Supply Lines

> "To bring the whole army over a thousand li, nothing is so important as economy in feeding."
> —ch. 2

A modern capital stack resembles an army's provisioning convoy:

- **Senior Debt** — the heavy wagons of grain. They feed the bulk of acquisition cost but move slowly and hate bad roads.

- **Subordinate Debt / Mezz** — light wagons, faster, carrying dried meat and tools. They fill gaps but demand higher tribute.

- **Preferred Equity** — the quartermasters who only speak to generals. They eat first in a crisis.

- **Common Equity** — the foot soldiers who fight for upside after everyone else is safe.

- **Contingency Reserves** — the spare mules and hidden caches along the march.

If any wagon fails, the line concertinas: speed stalls, morale drops, and the enemy—vacancy, rising rates, cap-ex surprises—can pick off units one by one. Protecting supply lines means three practices:

1. **Diversify Sources** — never depend on a single lender class or investor clique.

2. **Sequence Wisely** — match each tranche's maturity to the project phase it funds.

3. **Stress-Test Ruthlessly** — run worst-case scenarios on cost of capital, draw delays, and covenant breaches before

term sheets are signed.

Just as Sun Tzu forbade long sieges because they devour rations, you must avoid funding plans that wobble if stabilization drifts by even six months.

---

2 Funding Sources: The Arsenal

> "He will win who, prepared himself, waits to take the
> enemy unprepared."
> —ch. 10

Being "prepared" today means knowing exactly which money to pull at which moment. Below are the principal weapons in the funding arsenal, their advantages, and the ambushes they hide.

2.1 Bank and Agency Debt

Strength: Cheapest rates, long amortization.
Ambush: Conservative underwriting; can collapse if DSCR dips below 1.25×.

2.2 Bridge and Debt-Fund Capital

Strength: Speed, high leverage, rehab draws.
Ambush: Variable rates and tight maturities—miss exit timing and default looms.

2.3 Hard Money

Strength: Approves on asset more than borrower; funds in days.
Ambush: Double-digit rates, heavy points; kills cash flow if hold drags.

2.4 Private Notes and Syndicated Equity

Strength: Negotiable terms, relationship-driven flexibility.
Ambush: Reputation risk; one mismanaged deal poisons your whole pond.

2.5 Crowdfunded Marketplace Capital

Strength: Taps retail investors at scale; marketing flywheel.
Ambush: SEC scrutiny, platform fees, public-facing disappointment if projections miss.

Know the quirks of each before the LOI stage so you can pivot when a lender's appetite changes overnight.

---

3 Private-Money Pitch Deck: One Page, Zero Fluff

> "In battle, there are but two methods of attack: the
> direct and the indirect; yet these two in combination
> give rise to an endless series of maneuvers."
> —ch. 5

Your one-page deck is a *direct* strike—simple enough to read in two minutes, intriguing enough to prompt diligence questions.

Length kills momentum; clarity compounds it. Build the page in nine blocks:

1. **Headline & Mission**
   "8% Target Cash Yield in Transit-Rich Workforce Housing." One sentence. No adjectives you wouldn't use in court.

2. **Deal Snapshot**
   • Units & vintage   • Purchase price   • Cap rate on in-place NOI   • Closing deadline.

3. **Operator Track Record**
   • Total doors bought   • Average realized IRR   • Defaults = 0. Bullet points only.

4. **Business Plan**
   • Light value-add: $7 k/door interiors, RUBS implementation, market-rate lease-up.
   • Exit year 5 at 5.75 % cap.

5. **Projected Returns**
   • Cash yield years 1 - 5: 6 % → 10 %   • Net equity multiple: 2.0×.

6. **Downside Protection**
   • DSCR break-even at 74 % occupancy.
   • Rate cap purchased at 6 %.

7. **Timeline & Milestones**
   • PSA signed → 30-day inspect → 60-day close → 90-day

first distribution.

8. **Ask & Structure**
   - Seeking $2.4 M pref equity at 8 % pref + 70/30 split over 12 %.
   - Minimum $100 k ticket.

9. **Contact & Compliance**
   - Direct line, Calendly link.
   - "506(c) for accredited investors only" in small print.

Everything else—full underwriting, rent comp grid, environmental report—waits behind an NDA. You captured attention; now momentum carries them into the data room.

---

4   The War Chest Rule: Three Months' Burn per Unit

> "The skillful soldier does not raise a second levy;
> neither are his supply wagons loaded more than twice."
> —ch. 2

Sun Tzu warns against repeated levies because scrambling for supplies mid-campaign slows the advance and signals weakness. In property warfare the levy is a capital call—humiliating, time-consuming, and value-destroying. The antidote is a **war chest** equal to three months of *total* burn per unit, set aside on day one and guarded like ammunition.

4.1　Define "Burn per Unit"

- Principal + interest (actual or interest-only)

- Taxes and insurance

- Utilities under owner meter

- Payroll or management fee

- Average maintenance and turnover cost

If the figure is $450 per unit per month, the reserve is $1,350 up front. On a 60-unit, that is $81 k. Investors balk at idle cash until you show them the casualty statistics of owners who ran at one month's burn and hit a winter boiler failure.

4.2　Funding the War Chest

- **Escrow at Closing** — easiest for discipline, part of equity raise.

- **Line-of-Credit Overlay** — arrange unsecured LOC equal to 50 % of war chest; draw only in crisis.

- **Cash-Flow Top-Up** — when occupancy exceeds budgets by 3 % for 90 consecutive days, siphon surplus into reserve until full.

4.3 Deployment Protocol

- **Red Lines** — dip into war chest only when DSCR < 1.0 *or* occupancy < 85 %.

- **Refill Trigger** — as soon as cash call ends, replenish within 60 days from operations or refinance proceeds.

- **Visibility** — monthly investor letter shows reserve balance; transparency stops panic.

Three months feels conservative—right up to the moment a slab leak floods eight units and the insurer rejects the first claim draft.

---

5 Sequencing Capital for Continuous Momentum

"In all fighting, the direct method may be used for joining battle, but indirect methods will be needed in order to secure victory."
—ch. 5

Direct capital gets you to closing; indirect capital keeps the rehab on schedule, the coffers calm, and the refinance smooth. Momentum dies when draws stall or equity deadlines clash with lender waiting periods. Sequence like this:

1. **Acquisition Debt & Equity** — locked 30 days pre-close.

2. **Rehab Escrow** — funded by bridge lender or separate
    cap-ex LLC; clear scope signed before close.

3. **Operating Reserve** — wired same day as equity, sits in
    interest-bearing account.

4. **Contingent Liquidity** — LOC or partner pledge
    documented, available within 48 hours.

5. **Permanent Take-Out** — term sheet or Fannie soft quote
    in hand by month six, subject to target DSCR.

If any step overlaps in a way that strains war chest or investor
confidence, re-order or renegotiate. Supply lines must never cross
and jam.

---

6   Monitoring the Health of Supply Lines

> "If the campaign is protracted, the resources of the
> State will not be equal to the strain."
> —ch. 2

You prevent protraction by tracking these pulse points weekly:

- **13-Week Cash-Flow Forecast** — rolling, updated every
  Friday.

- **Reserve Coverage Ratio** — war-chest balance ÷ monthly
  burn; red alert at < 2.5.

- **Covenant Cushion** — actual DSCR minus covenant DSCR.

- **Draw Turnaround Time** — days between cap-ex submission and funding; goal < 10.

- **Lender Sentiment Score** — subjective 1-5 after each call; plummeting score signals refinancing early.

A convoy captain walked the line each dusk inspecting wheel rims; you walk your QuickBooks and lender portals each week, hunting wobble before collapse.

---

7 Case Study: Two Supply Lines, Two Outcomes

Alpha Capital raised just enough equity, skipped war chest, and relied on optimistic rent bumps. Month 11 a hailstorm shattered roofs and vacancy hit 40 %. Insurance check came 90 days later; mezz lender accelerated. Forced sale at 60 cents on the dollar.

Bravo Holdings baked in three months' burn, plus LOC equal to another month. Same storm, same insurance delay. They fronted roof repair from reserves, offered discounted rents to retain tenants, and still met debt service. Refinance year 3 returned full capital to investors.

Difference: supply lines.

> "The general who wins makes many calculations in
> his temple before the battle is fought."
> —ch. 1

The reserve calculation is your temple math.

---

8   Building Relationships that Guard Momentum

Money moves along human channels. Keep those channels clear:

- **Quarterly Lender Calls** — share occupancy, cap-ex progress, and trailing-twelve NOI. Proactive truth buys grace when hiccups come.

- **Investor "Heartbeat" Emails** — short updates every 30 days; radio silence breeds rumor.

- **Vendor Payment Discipline** — pay contractors net-30 or faster; a starved vendor can lien your project and freeze draws.

- **Back-Up Bench** — two alternate lenders, two alternate GCs, one alternate PM signed up before you need them.

Sun Tzu rotated fresh troops to the front to let others rest; your bench keeps operations fluid when a provider flames out.

---

9 Negotiation Tactics to Protect Capital Terms

"When you surround an army, leave an outlet free."
—ch. 7

Your capital partners are not enemies, but they are cautious. Give them an "outlet"—protections that satisfy their risk committees without crippling your upside.

- **Rate Caps** — you pay for them; lenders relax DSCR thresholds.

- **Preferred Return Escrows** — small initial escrow can convince equity of seriousness.

- **Waterfall Flex** — step-down promote if IRR drops below target; encourages patience in slow markets.

- **Conversion Clauses** — mezz converts to equity instead of default—saves the asset, salvages relationships.

Concede where it costs least; defend where future upside compels most.

---

10 Momentum Mindset: Expect the Ghost Army

"Appear at points which the enemy must hasten to defend; march swiftly to places where you are not expected."
—ch. 6

In capital terms, the ghost army is the surprise expense, the rate spike, the frozen draws. Assume they will appear. Drill:

1. **Rate-Shock Simulation** — +300 bps on SOFR; does DSCR hold?

2. **Exit-Cap Stretch** — +100 bps at sale; IRR still $\geq$ target?

3. **Draw Freeze** — 60-day funding gap; war chest covers?

4. **Insurance Denial** — self-fund deductible; LOC ready?

Run these quarterly. Each pass strengthens muscle memory, the same way marching through mountain passes conditioned ancient troops.

---

11 Putting It All Together: A Funding Checklist

Before PSA:

- Identify at least two senior-debt paths, two equity funnels.

- Draft initial 13-week cash-flow model with worst-case rehab draw schedule.

Before LOI expires:

- Confirm lender term sheet that matches rehab scope.

- Prepare one-page pitch deck; schedule investor webinars.

At contract:

- Build full pro forma with reserve allocation ≥ three months' burn.

- Open escrow account for reserves; wire first tranche.

30 days prior to close:

- Lock rate-cap strategy; budget premium.

- Secure LOC or written partner backstop letter.

Closing week:

- Fund war chest.

- Flip switch on weekly cash-flow dashboard.

First 90 days post-close:

- Confirm draw cadence meets schedule.

- Publish three "heartbeat" updates.

- Re-forecast DSCR with actual rents.

Momentum secured. Campaign marches.

---

12   Conclusion: Speed Controlled by Liquidity

> "Speed is the essence of war."
> —ch. 11

Speed in property war is not reckless sprinting; it is the confidence to move swiftly *because* your supply lines can absorb friction. You buy right, rehab on schedule, stabilize early, refinance without groveling, and distribute on the promise date. Investors re-up, lenders compete, and brokers funnel you the next off-market lead.

Guard the capital stack like archers guarding the baggage wagons. Build a war chest no storm can empty. Speak in one-page decks that cut through noise. And march, always march, with liquidity at your back and momentum rolling under your boots.

---

[1] This quotation is a commonly cited paraphrase of Sun Tzu's focus on logistics in chapter 2. The spirit—and the warning—are directly his: without well-protected supplies, the campaign dies long before the battlefield.

Chapter 6

Command & Control: Project Management

> "The general who advances without coveting fame
> and retreats without fearing disgrace, whose only
> thought is to protect his country and do good service
> for his sovereign, is the jewel of the kingdom."
> —*Sun Tzu, The Art of War*, ch. 10

In real-estate operations the "country" is your balance sheet and the "sovereign" is the investor who entrusted you with capital. You become that jewel not through charisma but through command and control: the deliberate orchestration of people, money, materials, and minutes from closing to cash-flow. This chapter forges three weapons that keep your campaigns short, decisive, and profitable:

- **A Gantt-lite roadmap**—lean enough to fit on one page yet detailed enough to kill ambiguity.

- **30-60-90-day battle rhythms** that push the roadmap forward at a tempo the market cannot outflank.

- **Decision gates**—hard stop-loss triggers that slice away sunk-cost bias before it grows malignant.

We close with a ground-truth case study: how a fourplex was stripped, renovated, leased, and refinanced in twelve weeks—a project most small landlords let sprawl across a year.

1 Why "Command & Control" Beats "Get It Done"

> "The enlightened ruler lays his plans well ahead; the
> good general cultivates his resources."
> —ch. 2

Plans alone do not win; resources alone do not either. Victory emerges where plan and resources meet a clock. Every day after close your cost of capital ticks, your insurance premium accrues, and your crew's motivation decays. Command & Control compresses that timeline, converting static pro forma into dynamic momentum.

- **Command** is the authority to allocate tasks, approve invoices, and redirect labor.

- **Control** is the visibility that tells you—instantly—whether today's allocation pushes the mission forward or drifts sideways.

Without both, a six-week paint-and-floors rehab mutates into a six-month money bleed. You avoid that fate by penciling a clear path before the first hammer swings.

2 Building the Gantt-Lite Roadmap

> "He will win who has military capacity and is not
> interfered with by the sovereign."
> —ch. 3

Military capacity today is the ability to see every dependency on a single sheet—no scrolling, no nested tabs, no twenty-column spreadsheets that only the analyst understands. The Gantt-lite roadmap is:

- A horizontal time axis no longer than ninety days for projects under fifty units.

- Never more than twelve task bars; each bar bundles micro-tasks you manage elsewhere.

- Color cues: green on track, yellow risk, red late.

2.1 Core Task Bars

1. **Demo / Trash-out**

2. **Structural & Rough-in** (framing, plumbing, electrical)

3. **Inspections & Permits**

4. **Mechanicals** (HVAC swap, water heaters)

5. **Exterior Envelope** (roof, windows, siding)

6. **Drywall & Paint**

7. **Finish Carpentry & Fixtures**

8. **Landscaping / Curb Appeal**

9. **Marketing Prep** (photos, listings)

10. **Lease-up / Pre-leasing**

11. **Punch-list & QA**

12. **Refinance or Sale**

Each bar has a start and finish date, baseline budget, and owner—*one* human, never "the team." Your software can be MS Project, Monday.com, Trello with timeline view, or a laminated poster marked by dry-erase pens; the medium matters less than the clarity.

2.2   Front-Load the Risk

Time bars that threaten critical path—permits, inspectors, long-lead materials—get placed first. Sun Tzu loaded supplies before marching; you load approvals before demo.

---

3   30-60-90-Day Battle Rhythms

> "Speed is the essence of war. Take advantage of the enemy's unreadiness; make your way by unexpected

routes."

—ch. 11

Speed without cadence becomes whiplash. The battle rhythm installs cadence: set-piece reviews at 30, 60, and 90 days (or 15, 30, 45 on micro-flips). Rhythm stabilizes expectations:

- **30-Day Checkpoint**

    o Demo complete, rough-in at least 25 %

    o Budget variance < 5 %

    o First draw funded

    o Updated schedule issued to trades

- **60-Day Checkpoint**

    o Rough-in inspections passed, drywall hanging

    o Lease-up marketing live

    o Budget variance < 7 %

    o Rate-lock confirmed for refinance

- **90-Day Checkpoint**

    o Punch-list under way, first unit rent-ready

- DSCR pro-forma validated with actual leases

- Final draw scheduled

- Appraisal ordered

These dates are immovable rocks. Trades, lenders, and property managers anchor their micro-tasks to them. If a delay pushes drywall inspection beyond the 60-day rock, Command & Control triggers an escalation meeting within twenty-four hours, not "sometime next week."

---

4   Decision Gates and Stop-Loss Triggers

> "There are roads that must not be followed, towns that must not be besieged, positions that must not be contested."
> —ch. 8

The sunk-cost fallacy whispers: "We already spent forty grand; we can't stop now." Commanders inoculate against the whisper by presetting gates—criteria that force a pause and reassessment.

4.1   Gate Types

- **Technical Gate** — mandatory inspection passes; if fail twice, escalate.

- **Financial Gate** — budget overrun > 10 % on any phase; freeze new purchase orders.

- **Schedule Gate** — milestone slips > 7 days; convene task-force.

- **Market Gate** — comp rents drop > 5 % in same ZIP; review exit strategy.

4.2 Writing the Trigger

A trigger must be measurable and binary.

Good: "Plumbing rough fails inspection twice → escalate."
Bad: "If plumbing seems behind schedule → escalate."

Escalation steps:

1. Field captain (GC) proposes root-cause within 24 h.

2. Project manager validates proposal, drafts options.

3. Sponsor decides: push, pivot, or pull plug.

Pulling plug may mean selling as-is, refinancing early, or mothballing half the scope. The discipline hurts less than losing another six figures while *hoping*.

5 Case Study — The 12-Week Fourplex Blitz

"Victorious warriors win first and then go to war."
—ch. 4

Asset — 1920s brick fourplex near a commuter rail stop; all units vacant, knob-and-tube wiring, collapsing porch. Purchased distressed for 65 % of ARV.

Objective — Complete gut rehab and lease-up inside a single quarter to capture spring rental surge and refinance before bridge lender's rate step-up.

5.1 Week 0: War-Room Setup

- Gantt-lite printed, signed by GC, electrician, lender.

- 3-month burn reserve funded (see previous chapter).

- Decision gates drafted: any inspection failure ×2, budget variance > 8 %, DSCR < 1.1 pre-lease.

- Daily stand-up call scheduled 7:30 a.m. with PM, GC, subs. Five minutes: wins, blockers, materials needed.

5.2 Weeks 1-4 (30-Day Rock)

- **Demo** stripped to studs in seven days.

- **Structural**: sister joists, replace porch piers.

- **Permits** filed Day 2; inspector walk-thru Day 10.

- **Rough-in** electrical, plumbing, HVAC parallelized—three crews, one floor each.

- Daily Slack photo uploads; budget burn 20 % (target 25 %).

- Marketing: drone exterior photos and "coming soon" landing page.

Checkpoint met Day 28—on time, under budget.

5.3 Weeks 5-8 (60-Day Rock)

- Rough-in inspections passed first attempt.

- Drywall hung and mudded by Day 45; paint starts Day 48.

- Cabinets pre-ordered claimed early-pay discount; delivered just-in-time Day 52.

- Landscaping rough cut; new rail station banner installed.

- First lease signed Day 56 at 5 % above pro forma.

- Trigger fired: roofing material delay threatened schedule +6 days—decision gate. GC proposed overtime weekend, sponsor approved $3 k premium, slip absorbed.

Checkpoint Day 59—variance 3 %, DSCR forecast 1.32.

5.4 Weeks 9-12 (90-Day Rock)

- Flooring, trim, appliances in, punch-list rolled.

- Appraisal ordered Day 70.

- Second lease Day 72, third Day 77. Last unit pre-leased Day 80 contingent on move-in Day 84.

- Final draw request Day 78, funded Day 82.

- Refinance closed Day 87; new loan paid off bridge, returned 50 % of investor equity.

- War chest still held 1.5 months' burn.

Total project—from keys to perm debt—twelve weeks. Net equity gain 35 % on forced appreciation; IRR annualized north of 100 %.

5.5 Post-Mortem

What made speed possible?

1. **Gantt-lite** gave every sub a visual scoreboard.

2. **Daily stand-ups** surfaced material delays before they hit schedule.

3. **Decision gates** punished drift before it metastasized.

4. **Reserve cash** removed "waiting on draws" excuse.

6   Tool Kit for Real-Time Command

> "Use the conquered foe to augment one's own
> strength."
> —ch. 2

The "conquered foe" is technology you already pay for; bend it to augment strength.

- **Shared Drive**—all permits, invoices, photos in date-stamped folders; audit trail equals lender confidence.

- **Group Chat**—Slack or WhatsApp labeled channels #demo, #hvac, #leasing; emojis mark status.

- **Daily Photo Protocol**—foreman posts timestamped shots; remote sponsors trust verify.

- **Color-coded Calendars**—Google Cal layered with inspection appointments in red, deliveries in blue.

- **Kanban Board**—Trello columns: Backlog, Doing, Review, Done. Subcontractors move cards; PM sees bottlenecks at a glance.

None of this needs exotic software. The power is in shared transparency.

7   Leadership and Communication Cadence

> "Regard your soldiers as your children, and they will
> follow you into the deepest valleys."
> —ch. 10

Trade crews are not children, but they crave respect, clarity, and quick payments. Command & Control meets those needs:

- **Kickoff Huddle**: donuts, scope walk, contingency plan. Sets tone.

- **End-of-Week Debrief**: 15 minutes Friday; celebrate win, share next week's blockers.

- **Prompt Pay**: ACH within 48 h of invoice and lien waiver; trades rearrange other jobs to stay on yours.

- **No-Blame Root Cause**: when gate triggers, you ask "what system allowed this," not "who is the fool."

The result: crews self-report issues early, lenders trust your numbers, investors feel the rhythm.

---

8   Common Project-Management Ambushes and How to Defuse

1. **Scope Creep**
   Counter: Any change order > $1 k pauses work until ROI

matrix signed.

2. **Permit Delays**
   Counter. Hire expeditor day one; build rapport at city desk; budget "official coffee fund."

3. **Material Shortage**
   Counter. Maintain two supplier quotes; store long-lead items in locked container on site.

4. **Crew No-Shows**
   Counter. Backup sub identified at bid stage, on-call retainer $500.

5. **Sunk-Cost Denial**
   Counter. Gate rule: if cumulative variance hits 15 %, mandatory disposition review with outside mentor.

---

9 From Command to Control: The Feedback Loop

"If you know neither the enemy nor yourself, you will succumb in every battle."
—ch. 3

Self-knowledge in project management is metrics:

- **Schedule Adherence** — planned days ÷ actual days. Target ≥ 0.9.

- **Budget Accuracy** — actual cost ÷ baseline cost. Target ≤ 1.05.

- **Quality Score** — defects at move-in per unit < 2.

- **Crew Stability** — turnover events per project ≤ 1.

After each project, feed these scores back into bidding algorithms, contingency factors, and timeline templates. Command evolves into mastery.

---

10 Conclusion: The Battle Ends at the Whiteboard

> "The general who wins a battle makes many calculations in his temple before the battle is fought."
> —ch. 1

Your "temple" is a whiteboard scrawled with a Gantt-lite roadmap. Your "calculations" are battle rhythms, decision gates, and war-chest math. When those elements align, a renovation transforms from a hazy hope into an executable operation. Crews know exactly what done looks like; capital partners catch no surprises; you, the general, sleep at night because the system, not adrenaline, drives success.

Twelve-week fourplex blitzes are not unicorns; they are the natural outcome of Command & Control executed with Sun Tzu's calm precision. Stand over your whiteboard, marker in hand, and plan—each bar, each gate, each rhythm. Victory will already be inked before the first nail is pulled.

Chapter 7

Open Ground: Class A Assets

"When the position is such that neither side will gain
by making the first move, it is called *open ground*."
— *Sun Tzu, The Art of War*, ch. 11

Class A property—fresh glass towers downtown, trophy
garden-style complexes in amenity-laden suburbs—fits Sun Tzu's
definition of *open ground*. Everyone sees the target. Everyone has
equal access. No moat, no secret path. On paper, the field looks
fair; in reality, only the commander who exploits speed, supply
discipline, and tactical surprise walks away with a yield worth
bragging about.

This chapter dissects Class A investing through that lens. We will
weigh its obvious **pros**—liquidity and friction-free tenants—against
its chronic **cons**—price wars and razor-thin spreads. Then we will
carve two flanking moves that bend open ground to your
advantage:

1. **Amenity stacking** — recombining lifestyle perks into a
   differentiation bundle rivals cannot copy overnight.

2. **ESG retrofits** — energy, sustainability, and health
   upgrades that subsidize themselves through capital-market
   discounts and tenant retention.

Master these plays and open ground becomes your hunting preserve, not a no-man's-land of compressed caps.

---

1   Why Class A Equals Open Ground

> "When the army faces the enemy on ground equally advantageous for both sides, it is called *open*."
> — ch. 10

Capital flows to clarity. Class A assets post the clearest signals:

- **Transparency** — financials audited, rent rolls digital, operating history deep.

- **Coverage** — brokers blast OM decks to global databases.

- **Market Depth** — institutional buyers, REITs, family offices all feel competent to bid.

The transparency slashes informational edge; the depth injects thousands of eyeballs. Like two armies on a broad plain, no party enjoys cliffs, woods, or chokepoints. The winner must therefore out-maneuver, not out-hide.

---

2   Pros: Liquidity and Tenants on Autopay

2.1   Liquidity

"Opportunities multiply as they are seized."
— ch. 5

Class A assets sell, refinance, or syndicate faster than any other grade. Reasons:

- **Debt Appetite** — agency lenders and life-co desks chase "balanced-sheet stabilizers."

- **Equity Channels** — pension funds mandate Class A for risk-adjusted compliance.

- **Valuation Benchmarks** — cap-rate comp sets update weekly; appraisers need no heroic assumptions.

Consequences:

- You can recycle equity sooner.

- Exit optionality increases leverage in negotiations.

- Market data verifies value, attracting passive investors.

2.2 Tenants on Autopay

"The clever combatant looks to the effect of combined energy."
— ch. 6

Class A renters skew professional, remote-enabled, or corporate-stipend. They:

- **Enroll in autopay at lease signing**; delinquency under 1 %.

- **Carry renter's insurance** without nudging; claim disputes minimal.

- **Renew if amenities support lifestyle**; turnover costs shrink.

The combined energy of low churn and smooth receivables stabilizes NOI, which compresses lender spreads further—momentum reinforcing momentum.

---

3 Cons: Price Wars and Thin Yields

> "No country has ever profited from prolonged warfare."
> — ch. 2

On open ground, campaigns drag because neither side dares overextend. Analogous drag in Class A:

- **Bidding Escalation** — auctions pry cap rates two-hundredths lower each round.

- **Yield Starvation** — stabilized cash-on-cash often < 4 % in gateway markets.

- **Cycle Vulnerability** — in recession, affluent renters double-up or buy discounted condos; vacancy spikes faster than in workforce stock.

Worse, improvement upside seems capped: countertops already quartz, pools already heated, gyms already mirror-walled. How does a commander break stalemate? By altering *terrain* without moving the asset.

---

4   Flanking Play #1: Amenity Stacking

> "The expert in battle moves the enemy, and is not
> moved by him."
> — ch. 6

If every tower sports a dog park and cowork lounge, those features cease to differentiate. Amenity stacking revives edge by **combining** perks into a user-flow others have not wired.

4.1   Designing the Stack

1. **Persona Mapping** — identify the core tenant archetype: e.g., "Singles working hybrid tech schedule and Tag-along pet owners."

2. **Daily Journey Audit** — list their morning-evening touchpoints.

3. **Bundle** two or three normal amenities plus one "category-breaker."

Example Stack:

- **Smart Locker Dry-Cleaning + Peloton Studio + Monthly TED-style Micro-Talks in Lounge**
  Rationale: Time-starved tenants value convenience, wellness, intellectual cachet. The talk series costs pennies (local entrepreneurs speak for exposure) yet seeds a vibe no adjacent tower matches.

4.2 Revenue Capture

- **Premium Units**: floors closest to amenity cluster command $75–$100 uplift.

- **Membership Model**: outside community pays subscription, offsetting upkeep.

- **Partnership Credits**: cowork brand sponsors fit-out for naming rights.

4.3 Execution Checklist

- Conduct tenant survey pre-renovation; test concept.

- Secure cap-budget; allocate 60 % build-out, 20 % tech, 20 % launch events.

- Pre-market with 3D renders; start waitlist before drywall.

- Track usage analytics; iterate quarterly.

By Year 2, stacked amenities raise NOI beyond what isolated features would. Competitors can copy one piece but not the integration narrative—your renters internalize the *lifestyle system*.

---

5   Flanking Play #2: ESG Retrofits

> "He will win who, prepared himself, waits to take the enemy unprepared."
> — ch. 10

Institutions pledge carbon and health targets faster than assets adjust. Retrofits seize that mismatch, turning cost center into capital-markets arbitrage.

5.1   Energy Upgrades

- **LED Conversion + Occupancy Sensors**

- **Variable Frequency Drives on HVAC Motors**

- **Solar Carport Arrays Feeding Common Meter**

These slash kWh 25 – 40 %, pushing utility expense ratios below underwriting norms. Some agencies (e.g., Fannie Mae Green Rewards) cut loan spreads 10 – 20 bps for 30 % savings.

5.2   Water & Waste

- **Low-flow Fixtures** — triple benefit: expense drop, green certification credits, marketing optics.

- **Stormwater Capture** — cisterns irrigate landscaping; qualifies for city fee discounts.

5.3   Health & Wellness

- **MERV-13 Filtration**, **Bipolar Ionization** for post-pandemic air standards.

- **Biophilic Design** — living walls, daylight corridors; proven to raise tenant satisfaction.

5.4   Certification Path

1. **ENERGY STAR** baseline.

2. **LEED for Operations** if capital budget low.

3. **WELL Building** for trophy assets seeking Fortune-500 corporate leases.

Spread savings + rent premium easily outpace retrofit payback inside five years. Competitors hesitate at upfront cost; you lock refinance terms early.

6 Financial Engineering on Open Ground

> "The general who thoroughly understands the
> advantages that accompany variation of tactics knows
> how to handle his troops."
> — ch. 8

Variation for Class A financing:

- **Green Bonds** — pair ESG retrofit with bond proceeds at lower coupon.

- **Forward-Rate Locks** — capture historically low long-term debt before retrofit completes.

- **Participation Loans** — senior lenders share in upside, let you lever to 80 % LTC without mezz.

Blend these with war-chest rules (Chapter 5) to keep supply lines liquid.

---

7 Risk Management Specific to Class A

> "He will conquer who has learnt the artifice of
> deviation."
> — ch. 7

- **Lease-Stagger** — ensure no more than 15 % of units roll in any single month; smooths vacancy whiplash in down-cycle.

- **Rent-to-Income Cap** — hold max ratio at 25 % to filter rent-stressed prospects even if screening score passes.

- **Pre-Underwritten Concessions** — budget one month free every two years; treat as CapEx, not afterthought.

Stop-loss triggers (Chapter 6) adapt: if asking rents trail comp average by > 5 % for 60 days, escalate marketing spend or price reposition.

---

8   Case Example — Turning a 2010 Class A into an ESG-Premium Cash Machine

Context: 320-unit mid-rise in Charlotte's light-rail corridor. Built 2010, Class A bones now B-plus vibes, 92 % occupied, trailing physical vacancy creeping from new construction nearby.

Strategy:

1. **Amenity Stack**

   - Convert underutilized racquetball court to *Creator Den*: podcast booths + green-screen studio.

   - Integrate parcel lockers with on-site "Cold Food Pantry" fridge units for grocery delivery.

- o Launch monthly art-night collab with local college; tenants plus public tickets.

2. **ESG Retrofit**

   - o Solar shade parking for 60 % stalls → 18 % common-area electricity offset.

   - o Upgrade chillers with heat-recovery; feed domestic hot water loop.

   - o Achieve LEED O+M Silver; Fannie green loan at 30 bps cut.

Outcome (Year 3):

- Operating expense drop $380 k/year.

- Effective rent uplift $110/month average.

- Re-appraisal cap rate same market benchmark, but NOI 19 % higher; valuation jump $14.1 M.

- IRR to investors 24 % versus 13 % base-case under classic light refresh.

Competitors still battle over concessions; open ground tilted subtly under their feet.

9   Common Ambushes and Counter-Tactics

1. **Over-Amenitizing**
   Counter: Pilot with one building wing; track utilization before full roll-out.

2. **Greenwashing Accusations**
   Counter: Publish third-party measurement & verification; share dashboards with residents.

3. **Asset Tax Reassessment After Retrofit**
   Counter: Negotiate abatement tied to environmental investment; many municipalities incentivize.

4. **Amenity Opex Overruns**
   Counter: Structure service contracts with cost-sharing—fitness brand staffs gym in exchange for membership upsell rights.

5. **Tenant Tech Fatigue**
   Counter: Keep apps unified; single sign-on for packages, events, maintenance.

---

10   Exit Plays on Open Ground

"Take advantage of the enemy's unreadiness; make your way by unexpected routes."
— ch. 11

Because Class A attracts sophisticated capital, exit creativity wins premium:

- **Recap with Core-Plus Fund** — sell 70 % interest, retain promote; harvest now, keep upside.

- **REIT Merger Arbitrage** — package several Class A's into OP units; trade tax deferral for liquidity.

- **Green Portfolio Roll-Up** — bundle multiple ESG-certified assets; valuation pops from scale and sustainability branding.

Move while rivals cling to single-tower dispositions.

---

11 Mindset: Leading on a Featureless Plain

"On open ground, one must simply seek to avoid
battle."
— ch. 11

Avoiding battle here means sidestepping the zero-sum auction. Operate where others hesitate:

- Blend lifestyle features earlier than trend watchers.

- Pre-qualify for green financing before it mainstreams.

- Treat talent (leasing agents, sustainability officers) as force multipliers, paying them like revenue creators, not janitors of status quo.

Do so and open ground no longer feels flat. It contours around your timing, creativity, and data discipline.

---

12 Conclusion

Sun Tzu's counsel for open ground condenses to one principle: *out-think what you cannot out-hide*. Class A property offers shimmering liquidity and disciplined tenants, but its visibility spawns merciless cap-rate compression. Crack stalemate by stacking amenities into cohesive lifestyles and by retrofitting sustainability ahead of the herd.

> "Hence that general is skillful in attack whose
> opponent does not know what to defend."
> — ch. 6

Competitors cannot defend rent rolls against savings they cannot yet achieve, nor defend commodity gyms against creator studios tenants Instagram for you. Shift the battlefield under their feet, and when acquisition committees finally notice, you will already be wiring refi proceeds to investors, scouting the next plain.

Chapter 8

Rough Ground: Class B/C Value-Adds

"When you come to a hill or a bank, occupy the sunny
side, with the slope on your right rear. Thus you will at
once act for the benefit of your soldiers and utilize the
natural advantages of the ground."
—*Sun Tzu, The Art of War*, ch. 7

"Ground which is reached through narrow gorges, and
from which we can only retire by tortuous paths, so
that a small force would suffice to crush the larger
force of the enemy, is called *precipitous.* It is a place
of fatal disadvantage."
—ch. 8

Sun Tzu's warnings about cliffs, gorges, and fatal disadvantage
translate almost one-for-one to Class B/C value-add real estate.
The cap rate dangling in front of you—8 percent, 9 percent,
sometimes double-digit—shines like easy treasure. Yet one
mis-step on rough ground and that same asset wallops a balance
sheet harder than any gleaming Class A tower ever could. Broken
windows, copper theft, vacancy spirals, insurance cancellations,
and contractor walk-offs are the modern equivalents of precipitous
cliffs and narrow passes. Master them and you will march where
timid capital will not tread; ignore them and gravity will test your
confidence with merciless speed.

This chapter drills into the terrain called Rough Ground:
neighborhoods in transition, assets built from the 1960s through

early 2000s, rents twenty to forty percent below new construction, deferred maintenance thick enough to swallow a novice budget. We map the opportunity, enumerate the dangers, and hand you a safety checklist forged in scar tissue—crime diagnostics, insurance land mines, contractor premiums—so you can collect the yield and leave the cliffs to the unprepared.

---

1   Why Rough Ground Tempts the Bold

> "Those who are skilled in war bring the enemy to the
> field of battle and are not brought there by him."
> —ch. 8

Value-add investors choose rough ground precisely because they can **bring** institutional capital onto a field it would usually avoid. They harvest four interlocking advantages:

1. **Elevated Cap Rates** – acquisition yields often 250–400 basis points higher than Class A comps in the same metro.

2. **Forced Appreciation** – every dollar of NOI recovered through rehab or management pops valuation by $12–18 depending on market cap.

3. **Low-Basis Risk Buffer** – when downturn hits, renters flee down the price ladder before they double-up. Your relative affordability cushions occupancy.

4. **Barrier to Competition** – big REITs fear headline risk; mom-and-pop landlords lack scale. Middle-tier sponsors

who professionalize rough ground face fewer bidders.

Yet every advantage is balanced by hazards that can drain cash faster than rent rolls fill.

---

2   Mapping Precipitous Cliffs: High-Risk Neighborhood Signals

> "We may distinguish six kinds of terrain, to wit: accessible ground, entangling ground, temporizing ground, narrow passes, precipitous heights, positions at a great distance from the enemy."
> —ch. 10

Class B/C corridors oscillate among Sun Tzu's "entangling," "narrow," and "precipitous" categories. You spot them through leading indicators before you ever order an appraisal:

- **Crime Gradient** – two adjacent census tracts can differ 300 percent in violent-crime rate. The steeper the gradient, the more likely negative migration or gang boundary tension sits a block away.

- **Insurance Zoning** – carriers quietly blacklist pockets after clusters of water claims, hailstorms, or civil unrest; quotes leap 50 percent crossing the street.

- **School-Rating Cliff** – a boundary shift that drops elementary rating from B to D slices resale pool and loan program eligibility.

- **Infrastructure Lag** – cracked sidewalks, half-lit streetlamps, storm drains clogged with leaves signal city budget neglect; capex solves only the parcel, not the block.

- **Political Optics** – council districts embroiled in recall battles stall permits; NIMBY coalitions may weaponize code enforcement after you take possession.

Your reconnaissance must overlay all five layers before LOI. The deal might still pencil, but now you know which elevations to fortify.

---

3   The Safety Checklist: Surviving the Cliffside

> "When you leave opponents a way of escape, they will prefer flight to death. Show them therein a path of retreat and leave them to their fate."
> —ch. 7

A checklist is that path of retreat—walk it and the enemy (unexpected loss) flees.

3.1   Crime Metrics

1. **Part I vs. Part II Ratio**
   Part I crimes (violent and major property) destabilize far more than petty theft. Pull twelve-month comps within quarter-mile and compare to five-year average. A ratio rising faster than citywide trend ≥ 10 percent flags

escalation.

2. **Response-Time Delta**
   Call the precinct's public-information officer: average
   minutes from dispatch to arrival. > 8 minutes in an urban
   core hints stretched patrols—expect slower trespass
   resolution.

3. **Night-Walk Protocol**
   Two passes—9 p.m. and 2 a.m.—within first week of
   diligence. Log loiter clusters, alley lighting, and audible
   gunfire. Digital stats never show the six-pack circle at the
   convenience-store steps.

4. **Leakage Map**
   Plot your property against sex-offender registry and
   major-case release halfway houses. Density > 1 per forty
   households requires enhanced tenant-screen marketing for
   workforce families.

Mitigations: LED floodlights, 360° cameras, license-plate readers
at lot entrances, and partial permieter fencing. Budget them before
purchase price finalization.

3.2 Insurance Red-Flags

> "Now the army forges ahead in pursuit of advantage
> without coveting fame, and retreats from danger
> without fearing disgrace."
> —ch. 12

Underwriters retreat from danger even faster.

1. **Roof Age & Pitch**
   Flat roofs older than fifteen years triple wind-hail premiums in Gulf or Tornado Alley states. Independent inspection + drone thermal scan determines replacement timeline.

2. **Copper / Galvanized Plumbing**
   Polybutylene or mixture piping triggers water-damage exclusions; retrofit allowance must sit in capex.

3. **Fifty-Year Electrical Panels**
   Zinsco, Federal Pacific, or split-bus panels can void fire coverage; carriers demand swap before binding.

4. **Prior Loss Runs**
   Seller's claims follow the address, not the owner, for five years. Too many water leaks and the "entire neighborhood" code pops up.

5. **Civil Unrest Surcharge**
   Since 2020, urban cores above a protest frequency threshold face riot-vandalism riders, adding up to ten cents per square foot.

Counter-tactics: negotiate in escrow for seller credit to replace systems that unlock standard coverage, or pool multiple properties into a blanket policy to dilute hotspot risk.

3.3   Contractor Premiums

Rough ground inflates labor cost even when wage books disagree.

- **Hazard Pay** – crews add 5–15 percent when tools need daytime lockboxes or off-duty cops.

- **Commute Surcharge** – subs refuse long drives without guarantee of full-day stacks; partial-unit turns become inefficient.

- **Municipal Inspection Chaos** – older stock triggers more reinspections; each re-visit multiplies idle hours.

- **Material Theft Buffer** – ten percent lumber shrinkage baked into bids; insist on fenced staging area.

Combat premiums by:

- *Block-booking* entire scope per trade—plumber hits all risers in one mobilization.

- *Local subcontractor alliances*—offer predictable pipeline, within four-mile radius, to secure loyalty discount.

- *Security deposit* paid to contractor for locked tool room you provide, reimbursed at punch-list.

4   Structuring the Capital Stack for Rough Ground

"The experienced soldier, once in motion, does not
suffer from drought; nor, once encamped, does he
ever experience want of supplies."
—ch. 7

On precipitous ground, liquidity equals oxygen. Stack capital with
wider margins:

- **Acquisition LTV** under 70 percent even when lender
  offers 80.

- **Capex Reserve** minimum 20 percent of project hard cost
  held in escrow, disbursed on percentage-of-completion, not
  invoices.

- **Interest Reserves** covering twelve months bridge debt.

- **Contingent Equity** letter of credit from sponsor or
  institutional JV, ready within five days for overruns.

Most failures trace back not to construction overruns but to
funding gaps that appear precisely when risk perception spikes
and fresh money flees.

5 Operational Doctrine on Rough Ground

5.1 Visible Presence

> "Appear at points which the enemy must hasten to
> defend; march swiftly to places he does not expect."
> —ch. 6

Criminals interpret empty leasing offices and dark breezeways as
invitations. Combat via:

- Leasing office open till 7 p.m. three nights a week—when
  shadows stretch.

- Branded golf cart patrols every two hours during rehab;
  residents see authority.

- Smart access control—pin code plus photo log; deter
  inside-job theft.

5.2 Tenant Mix Engineering

In B/C stock, one rogue tenant unravels morale floor by floor.
Weight screening criteria toward **predictable payers**: municipal
employees, hospital staff, logistics-hub workers commuting odd
shifts. Build partnerships with HR departments; they pre-vet
income reliability.

5.3 Maintenance SLAs

Speed neutralizes rumor. Publish "24-Hour Promise" for
emergency work orders, 72 hours for routine. Track with cloud

system accessible by residents; transparency discourages furnace-filter social-media rants.

---

6 Force-Multipliers: Community and Civic Levers

> "The support of the people is essential to victory."
> —ch. 12

Civic goodwill lowers enforcement friction.

- **Adopt-a-Block** litter sweeps once a month; public works department notices, speeds pothole repair requests.

- **Police Coffee Fridays**—invite beat officers for free coffee in clubhouse; build cellphone rapport for off-duty security hires.

- **Local Non-Profit Grants**—apply for energy-efficiency or lead-abatement funds; offsets capital, reframes project narrative.

A single council-member endorsement can shave inspection response days and insulate against anti-landlord media spikes when you issue eviction notices to chronic non-payers.

---

7 Advanced Risk Analytics: Dynamic Cliff Monitoring

Sun Tzu relied on scouts and signal fires; you wield data.

- **Weekly Crime Feed** — JSON scrape of city incident log; trigger security vendor patrol escalation if burglary within 500 feet.

- **Lease Fall-Out Radar** — dashboard flags if pending renewals in two consecutive stairwells exceed 30 percent; may signal localized gang pressure.

- **Insurance-Score Drift** — quarterly broker check for AM Best downgrades; downgrade trend signals premium spike at next renewal.

- **Social-Media Sentiment** — natural-language scan of property hashtag; early detection of tenant unrest.

With dynamic alerts, you adjust capex or marketing before NOI leakage shows in financials.

---

8 Case Study: Conquering the Cliff—From 60 Percent Occupancy to 95 Percent in 14 Months

Asset: 168-unit 1975-vintage, stucco walk-up outside Phoenix. Purchase cap 9.2 percent, violent-crime rate 2.3× metro average.

Safety plan deployed:

1. **Crime mitigation**

   - Installed 40 LED pole lights; cut night-time incidents 70 percent YOY.

   - Hired bilingual former Marine as resident security manager; $45 k salary offset by theft reduction.

2. **Insurance pivot**

   - Re-pitched carrier after plumbing re-pipe; premium dropped from $480 to $310 per door.

   - Captured 35 bps on refinance by presenting five-year claims-free forecast.

3. **Contractor cost containment**

   - Signed three-year master service agreement with local GC; locked labor at 2023 rates with CPI cap 3 percent.

   - Paid 50 percent of final invoice in Bitcoin equivalent—GC's speculative upside traded for 4 percent line-item discount.

Results:

- Year-one NOI lifted 41 percent.

- Appraisal cap 6.5 percent; valuation leap $9.8 million.

- Refi returned 112 percent of investor equity; IRR 33 percent.

Rough ground became a stairway to fortified cash flow.

---

9 Mental Models: Fear Discipline vs. Fear Paralysis

> "He will win who knows when to fight and when not to fight."
> —ch. 3

Use fear to sharpen, not freeze:

- **Fear Discipline** identifies every hazard and prices it.

- **Fear Paralysis** conflates hazard with impossibility and walks away from asymmetric upside.

Ask: *Is this danger priced into the cap rate and can I mitigate cheaper than the discount?* If the answer is yes, march; if no, hold fire.

---

10 Conclusion: The Edge at the Cliff

> "Hence policy is based on *circumstances*."
> —ch. 8

Class B/C value-add is a circumstantial battlefield where cap-rate tailwinds fight head-wind risks minute by minute. You win by mapping every precipice, drilling through the safety checklist, and deploying force multipliers that turn a precarious foothold into commanding height.

Step onto rough ground with Sun Tzu's clarity. Illuminate crime data, interrogate insurers, over-capitalize reserves, pay contractors like allies not mercenaries, and court city hall until they cheer your ribbon-cutting. Then the cliffs cease to threaten; they become your fortress walls, keeping timid money out while your cash returns compound safely inside.

Chapter 9

Key Ground: Transit-Oriented & Infill Gems

> "Ground which forms the key to three contiguous
> states… Whoever occupies it first has most of the
> Empire at his command."
> —*Sun Tzu, The Art of War*, ch. 10

In Sun Tzu's lexicon **key ground** is territory whose control unlocks the movement of armies, food, and information across a whole region. Modern analogues are parcels knotted to high-capacity transit lines and vacant niches inside built-out urban grids—sites whose capture channels commuter flow, consumer dollars, and political goodwill straight into your rent roll.

Class A towers may dazzle, Class B/C rehabs may cash-flow, but transit-oriented and infill gems compound **both** advantages while slashing the vacancy risk that torpedoes peripheral assets during downturns. This chapter equips you to scout, attack, and hold key ground. We will map how transit lines mirror ancient supply routes, then drill the entitlement hacks—lobbying councils, forging win–win deals—that pry approvals loose long before slower rivals finish their first neighborhood coffee-chat.

1 Why Transit Equals Supply Routes

> "The line of supply must be kept unbroken; if we can secure the road, the enemy's provisions will fail."
> —ch. 6

Sun Tzu understood that armies starve when wagons stall; cities today hemorrhage productivity when buses, subways, bikeways, and highways choke. Residents will trade square-footage, countertop grade—even school district—if the trade buys them **time**. Land within a ten-minute walk or five-minute bike of reliable transit converts time into value at a ratio no marble lobby can match.

1.1 Embedded Demand Engines

- **Job Access Multiplier**   Every added rail station within thirty minutes of CBD lifts average wage potential. Higher wages support higher rents.

- **Car-Light Households**   Millennials, singles, retirees shed parking stalls; you monetize land twice by building units instead of asphalt.

- **Corporate Site-Selection**   Tech and health-care firms chase transit corridors to widen talent radius without raising salaries. Their leases anchor ground-floor retail or absorb office incubator space inside mixed-use designs.

1.2 Liquidity Premium

Lenders, REITs, and institutional funds model "transit adjacency" as its own risk bucket. Lower vacancy volatility during recessions justifies sharper cap rates and larger loan proceeds. Your equity IRR benefits both at entry and at exit.

---

2 Reconnaissance: Reading the map like a Quartermaster

> "He who knows the roads is able to turn the enemy
> into confusion."
> —ch. 7

Modern reconnaissance merges GIS layers with boot-leather walks. Follow a four-step loop:

1. **Overlay** future transit extensions on current parcel map. Metropolitan Planning Organizations publish five-, ten-, and twenty-year capital plans; they change, but budget allocations serve as probability markers.

2. **Clock** real-time headways—peak and off-peak—by standing on platforms. A line scheduled every ten minutes but slipping to twenty negates premium rent.

3. **Track** last-mile gap. Is the sidewalk continuous? Are bike lanes protected or painted? Measure the *felt* commute, not Google's theoretical.

4. **Listen** inside morning trains. Commuter chatter about
    safety, lateness, or fare hikes foretells migration trends
    better than census lag.

Confirm that the route is not only funded but *socially entrenched*.
A bus route can vanish with city-council whim; light rail anchored
by sunk steel almost never does.

---

3   Acquisition Tactics on Key Ground

> "First seize what he holds dear; then he will be
> amenable to your will."
> —ch. 11

What sellers hold dear on key ground is **certainty**. They fear two
nightmares: (1) the buyer will retrade after discovering zoning
constraints, or (2) the deal will die waiting for entitlements while
rates rise. Flip both fears into negotiation edge.

3.1   Certainty Premium Strategy

Offer slightly under whisper price **plus** a signed exhibit showing
(a) pre-application meeting with planning staff logged; (b)
traffic-impact letter from transit agency stating "no adverse effect."
Documented preparedness often beats higher-priced LOIs that still
need six months of study.

3.2   Zero-Parking Valuation Arbitrage

Calculate what the land under surface stalls could fetch as additional units. If code allows a reduced ratio because of transit proximity, share half that gain with the seller via price bump contingent on secured variance. The seller sees upside; you still bank the other half when variance passes.

3.3 Option with Rolling Close

For assemblages, control the pivot parcel first through option; trigger successive purchases as entitlements clear sub-phases. Limits dead carry and shows small owners you respect their timeline.

---

4 Entitlement Hacks: Lobbying Local Councils

> "The general who wins the support of his sovereign
> can wage war even with a small army."
> —ch. 11

In entitlement war the **sovereign** is the city council or planning commission. Their blessings open density gates and kill parking ratios. Unlike by-right suburbs, transit districts are political fabric: neighbors, nonprofit coalitions, mobility advocates. You must build a coalition before the NIMBYs organize.

4.1 Intelligence Gathering

- **Voting History Grid** Study every council member's record on up-zones, affordable-housing mandates, climate initiatives. You'll predict which talking points sway.

- **Committee Power** Actual veto often sits in subcommittee. Attend two meetings and talk to staff—they whisper the chair's pet concerns.

- **Neighborhood Captains** Identify block-association leaders who mobilize dozens of comment letters with one email.

4.2 Message Crafting

Sun Tzu preached aligning army goals with **Moral Law**—people's sentiment. Craft messages that triangulate three moral vectors:

1. **Mobility Equity** Frame project as widening access to jobs for non-drivers.

2. **Climate Resilience** Show GHG reductions via TDM plan—bike lockers, car-share pods.

3. **Local Business Lift** Cite studies: "Every 100 residents within walking distance adds \$X to main-street revenue."

Tie each to measurable deliverables. Vague good intentions invite amendments that drain yield.

4.3 Soft-Power Tactics

- **Pre-Application Tours** Walk council through derelict lot, present renderings from same vantage. People defend what they visualize.

- **Third-Party Champions**   Secure letter from transit authority praising joint-development synergy; council weighs agency credibility heavily.

- **Data Gift**   Offer to fund a micro-mobility count or traffic-calming design that the city lacked budget to run; you become solution, not petitioner.

4.4   Hard-Power Negotiables

Sometimes moral suasion fails. Prepare quid pro quo:

- **Public Easement Dedication**   Donate five-foot strip for wider sidewalk; unlock 10 ft extra height via form-based code incentive.

- **Inclusionary Set-Aside**   If council fixates on affordable units, run underwriting for 10–15 % at 60 % AMI. Cover NOI gap with tax-increment financing or volume-cap bonds.

- **Transit-Pass Subsidy**   Offer annual passes for residents; agencies often discount bulk 40 %. Cost less than building excess parking.

You win by pricing each giveback **before** it lands on negotiation table, just as Sun Tzu stocked grain before besieging a city.

---

5 Win-Win Community Deals

> "Hence the enlightened ruler is heedful, and the good general full of caution."
> —ch. 12

Caution does not mean timidity. It means structuring deals where each stakeholder points to a line item they gained, killing future lawsuits.

5.1 Community Land Trust (CLT) Partnerships

Allocate ground-floor condo to CLT at below-market price; they secure perpetual affordability, you secure density bonus plus philanthropic PR. Finance discount with PACE loan on rooftop solar you wanted anyway.

5.2 Public Realm Enhancements

Commission a pocket park maintained by HOA. City waives setback, letting you recapture FAR vertically. Tenants gain a green view; city press releases its park-per-capita achievement.

5.3 Local Hiring Pledges

Set target: 25 % construction hours go to neighborhood residents. Workforce agencies supply trainees, lowering your labor cost curve by offset grants and derisking permit schedule.

5.4 Art & History Integration

If parcel sits in cultural district, reserve lobby mural wall for rotating local artists. Minimal capex, but historical commission now testifies on your behalf.

---

6 Design Principles for Transit-Oriented Value

> "He will win who adjusts his plan to circumstance."
> —ch. 8

Transit adjacency changes design math:

- **Active Frontage**   Zero-setback retail fosters walkable edges; double internal corridor means dual-exposure units lease first.

- **Vertical Circulation Efficiency**   More studios and one-beds require more elevators per square foot; budget energy-recovering motors to offset.

- **Micromobility Storage**   Secure e-bike cages with charge outlets; insurance prefers separated battery room.

- **Noise Mitigation**   Triple glazing and off-sleep fan speeds ensure riders don't hear platforms at 5 a.m.—cheap layer to defend rental premium.

Architects seldom ride the line; you should ride it with them before schematic design freeze.

7   Capital Stack Engineering on Key Ground

> "Taking a state whole is superior; destroying it is
> inferior."
> —ch. 3

Your goal is *whole* value: refinance or sale at stabilized NOI with entitlement upside baked in.

- **Pre-Dev Bridge**   Short-term, interest-only, sized off appraised land value *plus* 60 % of as-entitled appraisal (if political probability high).

- **Mezz with Conversion Feature**   If loan-to-cost gap remains, mezz that converts to preferred equity at construction closing; avoids double due diligence.

- **Transit-Agency Grants**   FTA TOD Pilot Program or state mobility funds can defray 5–10 % of soft costs; treat as quasi-equity.

- **Green Construction Debt**   ESG alignment reduces spreads; pair with PV arrays shading platform-view roof.

Exit scenarios: (a) core-plus buyer acquires fully stabilized asset; (b) REIT forward-commits at TCO plus margin; (c) REIT buys you out of operating partnership post-CO with cap-rate kicker for entitled air-rights phase two.

8   Risk Matrix and Mitigation

> "He will conquer who has prepared himself, and waits
> to take the enemy unprepared."
> —ch. 6

Risk | Mitigation
 Transit funding diverted   → secure letter of no-objection +
escrow milestone reimbursements
 Ridership decline post-pandemic   → diversify by adding
micro-warehousing for e-commerce tenants who value same-day
rail freight access
 Political flip hostility   → institutionalize community benefits
agreement recorded against deed; new council cannot reverse
 Construction inflation   → early GMP with material escalation
clause pegged to PPI; hedge steel futures for major quantities
 Interest-rate spike before refinance   → purchase forward-starting
swap at loan-application stage

---

9   Case Narrative: From Brownfield to Commuter Keystone

> "The quality of decision is like the well-timed swoop of
> a falcon."
> —ch. 5

Site   Eight-acre decommissioned railyard, two blocks from
proposed commuter-rail infill station in Dallas-Fort Worth corridor.

Year 0   Sponsor options parcel for $4 M, 18-month term. Spends $450 k on Phase II cleanup & station-area planning charrette co-hosted with city.

Year 1   State legislature earmarks last-mile funding; sponsor files rezoning to mixed-use TOD overlay. Offers city easement for pedestrian bridge across track.

Year 2   Council approves 120 ft height, 0.9 parking ratio. Sponsor closes land with bridge loan at 60 % LTC. LP equity oversubscribed after green bonds offered to pension fund.

Construction   Executed 348 apartments, 30 k sf retail, 60 k sf medical office. Local artists funded by 1 % budget ordinance clad façade with kinetic panels referencing rail history.

Stabilization Year 5   Occupancy 97 %, average rent 18 % above pro forma due to walkable grocery tenant. Sponsor sells to core REIT at 4.9 % cap, yielding 32 % IRR.

Brownfield became keystone because sponsor seized supply route *before* tracks laid, aligning every negotiation piece—council, agency, community—into a single line of advance.

---

10   Mindset: Steward, Not Speculator

> "Treat the people as your beloved children, and they
> will follow you into the deepest valley."
> —ch. 10

Transit-oriented infill draws civic passion. Enter as steward and the community supplies political capital; enter as flip artist and they mobilize lawsuits. Stewardship profits by:

- Transparent construction timelines posted at station kiosks.

- Resident discount on platform retail coffee joint.

- Yearly scholarship funded from asset ops for neighborhood STEM students.

Stewardship secures nine-figure exits by shrinking entitlement friction and vacancy loss—a yield invisible in the first spreadsheet but glaring after year three.

---

11   Conclusion: Hold the Keys, Command the Routes

Key ground is rare: rail nodes, bus-rapid-transit platforms, river ferry docks, micro-mobility corridors that cannot move without billions and decades. **Whoever controls it commands housing supply elasticity, tenant quality, and—ultimately—city growth narrative.**

> "He who occupies the key ground first and awaits the enemy there will be at ease."
> —ch. 10

Occupy with diligence: scout routes, price givebacks, lock grain (capital), win the sovereign (council), and feed the people (community benefits). Then, even when markets gyrate, trains will keep unloading tenants at your doorstep, and your rents will march on like steel wheels singing at dawn.

Chapter 10

Variations in Tactics: Riding the Market Cycle

> "Now an army may be likened to water, for just as
> flowing water avoids the heights and hastens to the
> lowlands, so an army avoids strength and strikes
> weakness."
> —*Sun Tzu, The Art of War*, ch. 6

Real-estate capital behaves like water. It rushes toward momentum during booms, evaporates when credit tightens, seeps quietly back into cracks before the next rush. Investors who treat the cycle as background noise end up dragged downstream; investors who bend tactics to each phase steer the river into irrigation channels that nourish portfolio growth in any weather.

This chapter converts Sun Tzu's doctrine of **variation in tactics** into a cycle-based playbook. We track four dominant phases—Expansion, Peak, Recession, Recovery—and prescribe two mindsets for each: **offensive buying** when conditions reward aggression, **defensive buying** when survival is the alpha. We then load three modular strategies you can bolt onto any phase: building **cash-flow fortresses**, switching to **distress-hunter mode**, and leading the **build-to-rent surge**.

By chapter's end you will carry a cycle compass, a tactical map, and a kitbag of maneuvers ready for the next yield drought or cap-rate crush. You will not guess the future; you will route around it.

1   Cycle Snapshot: Reading the Battlefield

> "He who knows the place and the time of the coming
> battle and the enemy's tactics will have victory."
> —ch. 7

Unlike equities, real estate hides its clock behind appraisal lags
and municipal permits. Yet four gauges flash cycle status months
before headlines confirm them:

- **Debt spread to 10-year Treasury** — Tight spreads under
  180–200 bps signal frenzied lending; blowouts > 300 bps
  foreshadow contraction.

- **CMBS delinquency rate** — When loans 30 days past due
  jump more than 1 ppt inside a quarter, recession pressure
  is building.

- **Construction-spending growth vs. absorption** — If
  supply outstrips net absorption by 30 % for three
  consecutive quarters, overbuild risk is cresting.

- **Cap-ex as share of NOI** — Rising ratios imply landlords
  investing to capture growth; plunging ratios often precede
  a buyer's market of deferred-maintenance bargains.

Lock these four dials on a dashboard; refresh monthly.
Trends—not single prints—warn you which maneuver to prepare.

2   Offensive vs. Defensive Buying

> *"In general, whoever is first in the field and awaits the coming of the enemy, will be fresh; whoever is second in the field and has to hasten into battle, will arrive exhausted."*
> *—Sun Tzu, ch. 6*

Offensive buying seizes the initiative: you move early, stake ground before rivals even muster, and capture rich returns where competition is still sparse. Defensive buying, by contrast, is a calculated entry only when hedges—fixed debt, cash reserves, downside protections—outweigh the lure of growth. Which stance you adopt depends on two shifting currents: market liquidity and price momentum.

During **Expansion***, capital flows freely and asset values climb steadily. That abundance of funding and positive price drift invites an offensive posture: lock in deals quickly, lean into leverage, and outrun slow-footed competitors.*

As the cycle reaches its **Peak***, financing remains available but lenders tighten terms, and valuations level off or wobble. Here, the prudent investor shifts to defense—seeking low-LTV, fixed-rate structures and demanding immediate cash-on-cash returns—rather than chasing marginal yield in a flattening market.*

When **Recession** *hits, liquidity evaporates and prices slide. Yet those armed with dry powder can strike with offensive force, buying distressed debt or assets at steep discounts. Investors without ready capital must sit it out or become distress hunters, prowling for forced-sale opportunities.*

*Finally, in **Recovery**, credit slowly returns and prices rebound from their lows. The sensible approach blends offense and defense: aggressively pursue mispriced openings, but anchor each purchase with conservative underwriting and clear exit plans. In this balanced pivot, you combine the vigor of early-cycle buying with the caution learned at the market's crest.*

---

3   Expansion-Phase Offensive: Speed and Leverage

> "Water shapes its course according to the nature of
> the ground."
> —ch. 6

When yields compress each quarter and lenders chase deals with ninety-day closings, your edge is **speed**. Offensive rules:

1. **Pre-negotiated credit lines**—rate caps locked, docs templated.

2. **Option rights** instead of long due-diligence PSAs; exercise only after lightning inspections.

3. **Leverage to ceiling on *stabilized* Class A or transit-oriented stock**, because cap-rate erosion outpaces default probability.

But leverage must pair with exit clarity: refinance or sale within two years, before the debt market asks harder questions.

4   Peak-Phase Defensive: Liquidity over IRR

> "Hold on to the height and sunlight; do not move
> unless the enemy does."
> —ch. 9

Signals: cap-rate movement flattens, rent growth stalls,
construction cranes bloom. Defensive buying rules:

1. **Low-LTV fixed debt**—60 % or less, interest-reserve
   funded.

2. **Cash-on-cash above 8 % on closing**—no pro-forma
   dreams.

3. **Stop-loss clause**—if cap-ex overrun exceeds contingency
   by 20 %, abort remaining scope rather than chase sunk
   costs.

Focus on assets shielded by supply barriers: infill lots with no new
permits, rent-controlled conversions where upside flows from
turnover rather than rent jumps.

5 Recession-Phase Offensive: Distress Hunter Mode

> "If the enemy leaves a door open, you must rush in."
> —ch. 11

Liquidity deserts, yet forced sellers surface: bridge-loan maturities, busted condos, absentee landlords exhausted by delinquency. Tactical kit:

- **Note purchasing**—acquire non-performing mortgages at 60–70 cents; foreclose or restructure.

- **Equity recap**—inject mezz capital into covenant-breached assets in exchange for GP control.

- **Tax-lien grabs**—counties unloading liens at pennies, turning into deed within twelve months.

Because credit is scarce, underwrite all-cash scenarios; excel at private debt syndication with equity conversion triggers.

---

6 Recovery-Phase Hybrid: Build-to-Rent Surge

> "Make forays in fertile ground in order to supply the army with food."
> —ch. 2

Pent-up household formation surges, yet for-sale inventory lags. Build-to-Rent (BTR) communities—purpose-built single-family rental clusters—feed demand. Keys:

1. **Land control during late recession**—finished lots at discounts.

2. **Vertical-integration JV with regional builder**—locked pricing before lumber rallies.

3. **Agency-backed take-out**—Freddie Mac's SFR portfolio program offers 30-year fixed on leased-up BTR at 75 % value.

BTR combines development upside with multi-family exit liquidity; capture spread early and harvest gate once cap-rates normalize.

---

7 Playbook Module #1: Cash-Flow Fortresses

> "Therefore those skilled in war bring the enemy to the field of battle and are not brought there by him."
> —ch. 6

A cash-flow fortress is an asset that self-funds reserves, distributions, and rate shocks without external cash infusions.

Blueprint

- **Debt**: 50–55 % LTV, amortizing, 10-year term.

- **DSCR**: Break-even at 70 % physical occupancy.

- **Reserves**: Six months OPEX + debt service locked in interest-bearing sidecar.

- **Tenant mix**: Needs-based demand—medical office, grocery-anchored retail, workforce multi-family near logistics hubs.

- **Lease structure**: staggered expirations, minimum 15 % annual rollover.

Cycle Use

- In expansion: buy fortresses mis-managed but structurally sound; raise rents, hold long.

- At peak: rotate hot-market equity into fortresses as defensive rebalance.

- In recession: fortresses survive lender scrutiny, letting you raid distressed peers.

- In recovery: refinance reserves into acquisition lines without touching distributions.

8   Playbook Module #2: Distress-Hunter Mode

"Move swiftly where he does not expect you."
—ch. 6

A distress hunter is a strike team that thrives amid broken covenants and capital calls.

Toolkit

1. **Locator grid**—live feeds of UCC filings, lis pendens, CMBS watch-list downgrades.

2. **Legal SWAT**—attorney retainer for rapid title & receivership petitions.

3. **Capital stack**—opportunistic fund or club syndicate with hard-stop 48-hour wiring protocol.

4. **Negotiation script**—focus on "speed and certainty" for lenders, "debt-wipe dignity" for owners.

5. **Re-tenant plan**—pre-signed LOIs with discount grocers, call centers, or public-sector agencies.

Cycle Use

- In expansion: keep dormant; gather relationships.

- At peak: test systems on small notes.

- In recession: deploy fully—target 3–4 add-ons per quarter.

- In recovery: exit cleaned assets to returning core-plus capital.

---

9   Playbook Module #3: Build-to-Rent Surge

"The clever combatant looks to the effect of combined energy—convergence of diverse forces."
—ch. 6

BTR fuses home-builder entitlements with multi-family operations.

Sequence

1. **Land-bank fringe lots two years pre-cycle lift**—adjacent to good schools, 30-minute commute to CBD.

2. **Entitlement sprint**—hire civil engineer who worked the comp project; reuse plan sets to cut six months.

3. **Phase builds**—deliver clusters of 30–40 units; lease while next pads pour.

4. **Tech stack**—prop-tech self-showings, centralized maintenance.

5. **Exit**—sell stabilized tranche to REIT or institutional SFR aggregator at 4.5–5.0 % cap while build costs still below

replacement post-inflation.

Risk Guardrails

- Fixed GMP with builder; allowance escalation capped at CPI + 2 %.

- Rate locks staged; backup float-down if Federal Reserve pivots.

- Bulk insurance negotiated across phases; avoid post-catastrophe premium spikes.

---

10   Decision Gates for Tactical Shifts

"There are five dangerous faults which may affect a general… recklessness, cowardice, hasty temper, over-solicitude for his men, and too great fondness for detail."
—ch. 8

Set quantitative gates to counsel against those faults.

- **Re-lever Gate**—only refinance upward if spread versus original debt ≥ 50 bps and DSCR stays > 1.5×.

- **Pause Gate**—halt acquisitions if cap-rate compression < 50 bps while construction cost index rises > 7 % YoY.

- **Distress Gate**—activate hunter mode when CMBS delinquency crosses 5 % and bridge default headlines appear.

- **BTR Gate**—begin lot offers when mortgage affordability index falls below 100 (households stretched).

- **Fortress Exit Gate**—consider sale if cap-rate difference between fortress and risk asset narrows under 75 bps; redeploy into next cycle's hunter fund.

Gates replace emotion with automation.

---

11   Case Walk-Through: Eight-Year Cycle, One Portfolio, Three Plays

Year 1–2 (Expansion)
Sponsor buys Class A TOD mid-rise at 5.2 % cap using 75 % LTV bridge. Sells within 24 months at 4.3 %, 2.1× equity.

Year 2–3 (Peak)
Net proceeds rotated into cash-flow fortress: 220-unit 2000-vintage, 60 % LTV, 8 % cash yield. Reserves set.

Year 4–5 (Recession)
CMBS wave hits. Sponsor's hunter fund acquires three defaulted notes at 65 % UPB. Uses war chest line for deposits. Forecloses, re-tenants.

Year 6–8 (Recovery to next Expansion)
 Launches BTR on land purchased from bank liquidation.
Stabilizes 200 cottages; sells to REIT at 4.8 % cap.

End-cycle outcome: blended IRR 28 %, zero capital calls, fortress
still spins distributions.

---

12 Psychology of Cycle Mastery

> "He who is prudent and lies in wait for an enemy who
> is not, will be victorious."
> —ch. 3

Prudence is not passivity. It is the discipline to bank relational
goodwill, cash reserves, and underwritten patience during feast so
that famine becomes harvest. Discipline decays under peer
pressure; a written playbook stapled to capital-call provisions,
lender convenants, and partner updates immunizes groupthink.

---

13 Conclusion: Variations as Strategic Anthem

Sun Tzu ends his chapter on variations with a warning:

> "The art of war teaches us to rely *not* on the likelihood
> of the enemy's not coming, but on our own readiness
> to receive him; *not* on the chance of his not attacking,
> but rather on the fact that we have made our position
> unassailable."
> —ch. 8

Cycles will turn, credit will evaporate, exuberance will return. Your job is not to out-predict but to out-prepare, rotating smoothly between offensive thrusts and defensive formations, deploying fortresses, hunter squads, and BTR battalions as conditions dictate. Practice the variations until switching feels instinctive, and the market, like Sun Tzu's defeated enemy, will find no seam to pierce.

Chapter 11

Nine Situations: Exit Strategies

> "The art of war recognizes nine varieties of ground:
> dispersive, facile, contentious, open, intersecting,
> serious, difficult, hemmed-in, and desperate.
> …The natural formation of the country is the soldier's
> best ally."
> —*Sun Tzu, The Art of War*, ch. 11

Sun Tzu names nine kinds of battlefield because each demands a distinct maneuver. Real-estate exits are no different. A portfolio marches across terrains that shift with interest rates, tenant sentiment, cap-ex surprise, and partner objectives; attempting to retreat by one route—"just list and sell"—is as naïve as leading cavalry through a swamp.

This chapter forges the parallel: **nine situations** become **seven exit archetypes** plus two holding extensions that bridge one exit into the next. Together they form an all-weather withdrawal doctrine. We will:

1. Translate Sun Tzu's terrain list into modern liquidity terrain.

2. Dissect the mechanics, timing triggers, and tax ripples of seven core exits—wholesale, flip, BRRRR recycle, equity syndication recap, §1031 exchange, Delaware statutory trust roll-up, and seller carry-back note sale.

3. Install the **decision matrix**—a quantitative "leave now"
    rule framed as

    **exit when rent-growth < (headline inflation –
    maintenance delta).**
    The formula locks emotional bias outside the command
    tent.

By page 134 you will possess a menu of retreats, redeployments,
and partial withdrawals—each rehearsed, costed, and coded into
lender covenants so that no surprise forces a fire-sale. Your troops
(capital) will never face a desperate flight; instead they pivot like
Sun Tzu's legion that *"makes a dash for advantageous position."*

---

1   Nine Terrains, Nine Liquidity Profiles

> "Ground which is of great advantage to either
> side—that is intersecting ground."
> —ch. 11

Replace *ground* with *capital stack*, *advantage* with *liquidity*.

1. **Dispersive ground** — multiple small partners, flexible
    deadlines: perfect for **wholesales** or **flips**.

2. **Facile ground** — stabilized Class A with agency debt:
    primed for **1031 trades**.

3. **Contentious ground** — rent-controlled, headline-risk
    asset: favors **seller carry-back** for a vetted buyer.

4. **Open ground** — transparent markets, tight spreads: ideal for **syndicate recap**.

5. **Intersecting ground** — mixed-use near civic corridor: **DST roll-up** harvests retail and residential under one trust.

6. **Serious ground** — bridge debt maturing amid rate spikes: calls for **BRRRR cash-out** or refinance.

7. **Difficult ground** — partially vacant C-class: **flip to local operator** or wholesale to specialist.

8. **Hemmed-in ground** — zoning constraints, union jurisdiction: exit by **equity recap** to deeper-pocket GP.

9. **Desperate ground** — covenant breach, negative NOI: **note sale** or short-sale handshake.

You may never walk every terrain, yet understanding all nine prevents paralysis when an unexpected ravine appears.

---

2 Exit Archetype #1 — Wholesale (Rapid Assignment)

> "Speed is the essence of war. Take advantage of the enemy's unreadiness; make your way by unexpected routes."
> —ch. 11

Purpose Capture option value and pass risk forward within thirty to sixty days.

Mechanics Contract property at discount; assign PSA to end-buyer for fee or close double escrow using transactional funding.

Ideal Terrain Vacant houses, small multifamily inherited by out-of-state owners, tax-sale surplus.

Risk Assignment outlawed in some states without license; seller blow-ups. Mitigate with earnest-money clause: refundable until inspection; escalates only at clear title.

Tax Income taxed as ordinary flip income, not capital gains. Recognize in the year of assignment.

When to Deploy Cycle early-recovery: distressed inventory high, retail buyers liquid. Or personal bandwidth scarce—wholesale flips capital without construction grind.

---

3 Exit Archetype #2 — Flip (Renovate and Retail)

> "To build a golden bridge for a retreating enemy is to
> leave him a way of escape."
> —paraphrase of ch. 7

The *enemy* is dated decor; the *bridge* is new granite.

Purpose Unlock retail-buyer pricing spread by cosmetic or structural rehab under twelve months.

Mechanics   Acquire with hard-money or private note, inject labor and design, stage for MLS or iBuyer platform.

Key Ratios   After-Repair-Value (ARV) ≥ 1.25 × (all-in cost). Carrying time ≤ 6 months.

Financing Watch   Hard-money points + realtor fees can swallow 20 % of resale price—budget ruthlessly.

Tax   Ordinary income again; shelter with S-corp salary splits or 20 % QBI deduction if qualifies.

When to Deploy   Expansion and early-peak when retail demand frantic and days-on-market low. In recession, flip risk spikes: hedge by pre-selling to landlord buyers.

---

4   Exit Archetype #3 — BRRRR (Refi, Return, Repeat)

> "The skilful employer of men will employ the wise man, the brave man, the covetous man, and the stupid man."
> —ch. 10

Skilful investors employ banks and private lenders sequentially.

Purpose   Re-cycle the same equity through buy-rehab-rent-refi-repeat; hold long, harvest cash-out tax-free.

Flow

1. **Bridge or private debt** acquires asset.

2. **Rehab** forces appreciation.

3. **Stabilize** at target DSCR.

4. **Agency cash-out refinance** returns initial capital + sometimes profit while retaining ownership.

Terrain Fit   B-C multifamily or scattered SFR with value-add opportunities; stable rent demand.

Tax   Cash-out from refinance is debt, not income—non-taxable (but deprec recapture later if sold).

Risk   Post-rehab appraisal shortfall; interest-rate hikes before perm debt; balloon risk. Hedge with rate-cap or forward lock.

Cycle Timing   Best in rising-or-flat cap-rate windows where appraisal gains not undone by cap expansion. During recession, DSCR hurdles tougher but purchase prices deeper—stress-test.

---

5   Exit Archetype #4 — Syndicate Recap (Partial Sale, Keep Promote)

> "If you know the enemy and know yourself, you need
> not fear the result of a hundred battles."
> —ch. 3

Enemy = equity trap; yourself = operating competence.

Purpose   Sell majority stake to incoming capital, pull chips, stay as GP with promote.

Mechanics   New syndicate or fund buys 60-90 % ownership at implied valuation. Existing partners cash out; operator signs performance-based asset-management contract.

Benefits   Realize gain without losing control; monetize sweat equity.

Tax   Sale portion triggers capital gains; remaining promote tax-deferred until final sale. Can layer §754 step-up for new LPs.

When to Use   Peak plateau: valuations high but continuing upside plausible. Also when moving from value-add to yield-harvest stage and desire co-invest.

---

6   Exit Archetype #5 — §1031 Exchange (Like-Kind Swap)

> "The rising of birds in their flight is the sign of an
> ambush. Startled beasts indicate that a tiger is in the
> forest."
> —ch. 9

Birds = IRS; ambush = tax on gains. Exchange is camouflage.

Purpose   Defer capital-gains and depreciation recapture by rolling proceeds into equal-or-greater property.

Rules (abridged)
Identify within 45 days, close within 180; replace both net equity
and debt. Must be investment property.

Terrain Fit   Long-held assets rich in phantom taxable gain;
geographical up-tier or consolidation.

Risks   Failed identification forces taxable boot; time crunch may
lure poor acquisition. Hedge with **reverse exchange** or
construction exchange to widen timing.

Cycle Timing   Favored mid-cycle when inventory plentiful and
valuations not overheated. Near peak, consider exchanging into
fortress assets to lock conservative yield.

---

7   Exit Archetype #6 — Delaware Statutory Trust (DST Roll-Up)

> "When the outlook is bright, bring it before their eyes;
> but tell them nothing so dreadful that they will lose
> hope."
> —ch. 11

DST offers bright outlook to passive investors fearing
toilets-and-tenants.

Purpose   Sell stabilized property into professionally sponsored
DST; small 1031 investors buy fractional interests. Sponsor
collects fee spread and often stays master tenant.

Mechanics   DST acquires fee-simple; IRS treats beneficial interests as direct real estate for 1031 purposes. Investors passive, non-recourse.

Benefits   Liquidity pool bigger than single buyer; execution premium 15–30 bps on cap rate. Good for mixed-use or institutional-grade multifamily.

Risks   Illiquid for DST investors; sponsor control heavy. Sponsor must underwrite loan limits (DSTs cannot refinance).

Cycle Timing   Late-cycle or early downturn: retail investors chase safety, low-volatility coupons.

---

8   Exit Archetype #7 — Seller Carry-Back Note Sale

> "When the enemy is in high spirits and eager for
> battle, do not engage him."
> —ch. 7

If buyers face high rates (enemy is eager?) you lull them with financing.

Purpose   Attract buyers when bank money expensive or property non-conforming. Seller converts equity into interest income, buyer secures leverage.

Mechanics   Seller holds first or second lien; negotiates term, amortization, balloon. Often 5–10-year I/O.

Benefits   Higher price for seller in exchange for time; installment-sale tax deferral. Capital gains recognized as payments received.

Risks   Default risk; impairment of future liquidity. Mitigate with cross-default clauses, personal guarantees, or collateral substitution rights.

Cycle Use   Downturn liquidity freeze. Instead of discounting price 15 %, hold note at 6 % and collect spread.

---

9   Decision Matrix: Knowing *When* to Exit

> "He will win who knows when to fight and when not to fight."
> —ch. 3

Exiting too late equals casualties; too early leaves loot on field. Install a formula that respects macro, micro, and property health:

Trigger = (Trailing-12 rent-growth) < (Headline CPI – Maintenance Delta)

- **Headline CPI** — Bureau of Labor Statistics urban All-Items YoY.

- **Maintenance Delta** — average annual cap-ex + opex inflation specific to asset (historical three-year mean).

If rent growth lags consumer inflation after adjusting for your rising upkeep, *real* cash flow shrinks. When the condition persists two consecutive quarters, your investment slips from "value accrual" ground to Sun Tzu's **contentious** or **hemmed-in** ground—fight extends resources without progress. Time to consult the nine exits.

Example:
- CPI = 4 %.
- Maintenance inflation (labor, materials) = 2 %.
- CPI − Δ = 2 %.

If your rent roll only climbs 1.4 %, red light flashes.

Secondary checks:

- DSCR forecast < 1.25× in two years,

- Cap-rate compression reversed 50 bps,

- War-chest reserve burns below four months.

Three reds? Trigger exit.

---

10   Stitching Exits into a Continuum

> "Make your way by unexpected routes and attack unguarded spots."
> —ch. 1

An elite commander chains exits: wholesale profit seeds BRRRR equity which later feeds DST roll-up. Example flow:

1. Wholesale five SFRs in Opportunity Zone; pocket $150 k.

2. Deploy as down-payment on 12-unit C-class (BRRRR). Cash-out $200 k in 18 months.

3. Exchange into 50-unit B-class via §1031; hold three years, raise NOI 25 %.

4. Sell via syndicate recap, keep 20 % promote.

5. Final disposition into DST to sunset management roles and collect coupon in semi-retirement.

Each hop neutralizes tax drag and matches personal bandwidth to life phase—a general's retirement back to the capital city.

---

11 Common Ambushes and Counter-Moves

- **Anchor Bias** — clinging to pro-forma IRR target although cycle turned.
  Counter: embed automated exit rule (rent vs CPI).

- **Tax Paranoia** — refusing to sell due to recapture; portfolio stagnates.
  Counter: model §1031 or installment sale paths early.

- **Refi Dependency** — BRRRR reliant on appraisal; market cools.
  Counter: keep backup sales comps ready; lock agency rate caps.

- **DST Over-Optimism** — sponsor underwrites low cap-ex; coupon erodes.
  Counter: perform your own condition assessment, demand repair escrows.

- **Carry-Back Moral Hazard** — buyer milks asset, stops paying.
  Counter: balloon at 24 months with personal guarantee; low LTV.

---

12   Psychology: Releasing the Arrow

> "The arrow shot from the bow flies swift and sure
> because of its discipline and the archer's calm."
> —paraphrase of ch. 12

Exiting tests ego; selling signals you were not immortal. Discipline demands a written **Exit Order of Battle** in your operating agreement:

1.   Quant triggers (rent vs CPI, DSCR).

2. Preferred sequence (1031 > recap > carry-back > broker sale).

3. Voting thresholds.

4. Broker engagement timeline.

With the order signed, you release the arrow when numbers dictate, not when gut rationalizes.

---

13   Conclusion: Victory Lies in the Withdrawal Plan

> "To secure ourselves against defeat lies in our own hands."
> —ch. 4

A property can be bought brilliantly, managed artfully, refinanced cunningly—and still bleed away hard-won equity if the exit falters. Draft your nine-exit playbook, plug the decision matrix into your financial dashboards, and rehearse paperwork for each route before the first LOI countersigned. Then, when rent growth loses to inflation, or maintenance swallows NOI, or city politics shifts against you, you will not freeze. You will choose, pivot, and march the liberated capital toward the next campaign—as calmly as Sun Tzu's army that saw every withdrawal weeks ahead of the enemy.

Chapter 12

Attack by Fire: Turnarounds & Special Situations

> "There are five ways of attacking with fire… The fire
> must be fanned when the wind is in your favor."
> —*Sun Tzu, The Art of War*, ch. 12

Sun Tzu's twelfth chapter is short, fierce, and often skipped by modern readers who believe incendiary arrows belong to antiquity. Big mistake. "Fire" in a real-estate portfolio is the deliberate, disciplined, and violent reshaping of a failing asset so it can rise from its own ashes. It is the turnaround toolkit: **restructuring debt, unleashing aggressive CapEx, and igniting a total rebrand**—all in a narrow window before lenders, tenants, or press flames consume enterprise value.

This chapter reframes Sun Tzu's five fire attacks into the language of property crises, then nails down a **30-day crisis-mode stabilization checklist**. The prose is hotter, the deadlines sharper, and the consequences—good and bad—show up on wire transfers, not smoke clouds. Master this doctrine and you will march into buildings (or balance sheets) others label "toxic," torch the dysfunctions, and leave with a scorched-clean canvas ready for value creation.

1   Why "Fire" Belongs in a Portfolio

> "Unhappy is the fate of one who tries to win his battles
> and succeed in his attacks without cultivating the spirit
> of enterprise; for the result is waste of time and
> general stagnation."
> —ch. 13

Enterprise is the willingness to pour resources into broken assets others flee. "Fire" projects—defaulted loans, half-empty malls, flood-wrecked multifamily, scandal-tarnished senior housing—look like charred timber. Yet every ember hides three asymmetries:

- **Mispriced Risk** Market panics on headlines; you underwrite on data.

- **Time Arbitrage** Competitors need board votes; your strike fund wires by Tuesday.

- **Narrative Delta** Public memory is short; a rebrand severs past stench, allowing cap-rate compression back to normal within thirty-six months.

Sun Tzu wrote that fire softens walls for infantry. In property, fire softens valuations so prepared capital can breach.

2   Translating the Five Fires

Sun Tzu lists: (1) burning soldiers, (2) supplies, (3) equipment, (4) arsenals, (5) communication routes. Cuing off that, the real-estate general picks five combustible targets:

1. **Debt Stack**   Balloon notes, covenant breaches, floating-rate ulcers.

2. **Deferred CapEx**   Roofs, plumbing, life-safety systems neglected.

3. **Brand Equity**   Online reviews, regulatory citations, press scandals.

4. **Stakeholder Morale**   On-site staff burnout, tenant rage, lender distrust.

5. **Cash-Flow Arteries**   Collections process, vendor terms, rent-setting logic.

Setting fire is not vandalism; it is controlled demolition of rot. The flames are legal documents, purchase orders, PR campaigns, and 5 a.m. inspections.

3 Fire #1—Restructuring Debt

"When the fire breaks out inside the enemy's camp,
respond at once with an attack from without."
—ch. 12

In turnaround language, "inside" is the lender's file room: payment delinquencies, technical default letters, maturing debt in frozen markets. The counter-attack:

1. **Inventory the Burn**

   - Balloon balance, accrued interest, late fees, swap breakage.

2. **Control the Narrative**

   - Email the asset manager before they call you; outline root cause, 30-day plan, new equity injection.

3. **Negotiate the Firebreak**

   - Forbearance (interest reserve pre-funded), A/B note split, rate-cap purchase in exchange for term extension. Show them your stack hydrant.

4. **Bring Replacement Water**

   - Bridge-to-re-stabilization lender, preferred-equity slug, or rescue partner that wires fast. Include make-whole for old lender on refi.

Lenders yield when shown credible capital and transparent cadence. They roast borrowers who hide.

---

4 Fire #2—Aggressive CapEx

> "The fire must be fanned when the wind is in your favor."
> —ch. 12

Wind = cost curve + vacancy tolerance. In crisis, both often align: building half-empty allows day-shift crews; suppliers discount bulk to move inventory. Attack sequence:

1. **Triage Inspection** Infrared roof scan, hydrostatic plumbing test, code-violation review.

2. **Scope Slash to Essentials** Life-safety first; curb-appeal second; amenity bling later.

3. **48-Hour Bidding Sprint** Invite three subs per trade, open book Zoom call, lock GMP with liquidated damages.

4. **Rolling Punch Lists** Turn crews finish stack by stack; units immediately staged and leased, funding next tranche.

5. **Cap-Ex Transparency** Weekly photo logs to lender and investors. Fire draws oxygen from secrecy; openness

smothers gossip.

The building must look and *smell* different within thirty days: dumpsters gone, lights bright, signage crisp.

---

5   Fire #3—Rebranding Blitz

> "The enlightened ruler lays his plans well ahead; the
> good general cultivates his resources."
> —ch. 2

Resource #1 is *perception.* Turnaround demands a fresh banner before final nails are driven.

Rebrand Playbook

- **Name Erasure**   Change property name, URL, and social handles concurrently; redirect old links.

- **Visual Shock**   New monument sign installed night before press release; tenants wake to new identity.

- **Story Frame**   Press kit: highlight capital improvement, sustainability pledge, local-hire plan. Quote city council ally.

- **Digital Flood**   Boosted geo-targeted ads and Google-My-Business posts; drown prior one-star reviews in a tide of new content.

- **Tenant Inclusion**   Hold courtyard breakfast with free swag; tenants become ambassadors, not skeptics.

Speed matters: weeks, not months. Brand surgery performed slowly only prolongs bleeding.

---

6   Psychology of Fire Command

> "If soldiers are punished before they have grown
> attached to you, they will not submit."
> —ch. 9

Crews, staff, tenants—treat them like draftees facing sudden conscription. Fire leadership steps:

- **Day-One Town Hall**   Explain crisis, timeline, what's in it for them.

- **Visible Sacrifice**   Sponsor on-site in hard hat at 6 a.m. day after closing.

- **Quick Wins**   Free high-speed Wi-Fi live within a week; staff phones replaced; tenants see change is real.

- **Fair Discipline**   Crew checks caught stealing tools fired publicly; message spreads.

Morale fuels throughput; fear alone melts teams.

7 Checklist—30-Day Crisis-Mode Stabilization

"When you are in difficult ground, keep steadily on the move."
—ch. 11

Pre-Close (T-48 hours)
• Wire working-capital reserve equal to 2 months OPEX
• Draft lender intro letter and attach 12-week action calendar
• Queue press-release template; embargo until signage swap

Day 1
• Locksite perimeter lighting schedule 5 p.m.-5 a.m.
• Conduct military-style unit census—photo ID every occupant; illegal tenants handled within 24 h
• Post emergency hotline answered by senior PM

Day 2-3
• Roof, electrical, plumbing inspections; red-tag any life-critical failure
• Issue staff retention bonuses with 50 % upfront, 50 % at Day 30
• Launch rebrand teaser on social: "Change is coming"

Day 4-7
• Secure forbearance or interest-reserve handshake; email to lender by Day 5 EOD
• Finalize CapEx GMP; order long-lead mechanicals
• Replace property-level email and voicemail greetings; old name purged

Day 8-14
 • Begin unit renovations in rolling blocks of four; list for
pre-leasing at market + modest premium
 • Host neighborhood association meet-and-greet; promise
security patrol report shares
 • Daily Slack stand-ups: GC, PM, owner; five-bullet limit

Day 15-21
 • Install new monument sign overnight; curtain-drop reveal with
local influencer livestream
 • Push Google review invite to satisfied legacy tenants; aim to
bury sub-3-star average
 • Collect first draw; verify lien waivers same day

Day 22-30
 • Achieve 90 % of "critical fixes" checklist; send lender photo deck
 • Release paid media story: "Historic Complex Gets $3 M Green
Overhaul"
 • Forward 60-day look-ahead schedule; target refinance appraisal
Day 120

Day 31, crisis phase ends; transition to normal value-add rhythm,
but momentum remains furnace-hot.

---

8   Case Study: 216-Unit "Ashyard" Reborn

The "Ashyard" (nickname earned after two arson events) sat 40 %
occupied, $2 M behind on taxes, with a $12 M CMBS note at 7 %
floating. Sponsor bought note for $6.8 M, accepted deed-in-lieu,
and pulled the fire switch:

- **Debt** — split note into A ($7 M, 4 % fixed) and B ($2 M PIK) with original lender.

- **CapEx** — $4 M GMP; 100 units turned in six months; solar carports shaved $120 k utility.

- **Rebrand** — "Phoenix Flats" launch party with city mayor; crime down 70 % YOY.

- **Exit** — Refi year two at 75 % LTC, valuation $22 M; IRR 38 %.

Sun Tzu's fire, modernized.

---

9 Guardrails: When *Not* to Strike the Match

> "He who is prudent and lies in wait for an enemy who
> is not, will be victorious."
> —ch. 3

Do **not** attack by fire when:

- CapEx escrow cannot reach at least 70 % completion before interest reserve dies.

- Lender servicing P&S forbids note splitting or cash-out.

- Municipal politics guarantee approvals drag beyond twelve months; you become the burned.

Patience until wind shifts beats bravado in no-win climates.

---

10 Exit Routes Post-Fire

Fire wins must crystallize quickly:

- **Refi Harvest**—12-18 months: DSCR jump yields tax-free return of capital.

- **Syndicate Recap**—Bring in core-plus fund to buy 80 % at new cap.

- **DST Sale**—Stabilized green features attract 1031 capital hungry for coupon.

- **Seller Carry-Back**—If rates soar, offer financing; lock price premium.

The asset should never linger lukewarm; either burn hot or sell while smoke still rises.

---

11 Conclusion: Wielding Fire Without Getting Burned

"Move not unless you see an advantage; use not your troops unless there is something to be gained."
—ch. 12

Fire is the sharpest blade in the investor's arsenal—quick, intimidating, final. Use it sparingly, prep obsessively, and extinguish ruthlessly once objectives met. Leave smoldering ruins for competitors to puzzle over while you march your revitalized asset, and freshly freed capital, toward the next battlefield Sun Tzu mapped twenty-five centuries ago.

Chapter 13

Using Spies: Data, Networks, Mentors

"What enables the wise sovereign and the good
general to strike and conquer,
 and achieve things beyond the reach of ordinary
men, is **foreknowledge**."
—*Sun Tzu, The Art of War*, ch. 13

The preceding chapters armed you with strategy, capital, and execution drills, yet every action still rests on one fragile assumption: *that the facts you used were true and complete.* Without real-time intelligence you become the commander who plans a river crossing unaware the enemy has sabotaged the bridge the night before. Sun Tzu solved the gap by hiring spies—men and women who slipped behind lines, listened, measured, bribed, and returned with insight no scout on horseback could ever gather.

Modern real-estate battlefields teem with secret signals every bit as decisive as an army's march route: off-market deeds recorded at 8:42 p.m., an obscure zoning memo buried on page 312 of a city-council agenda, a prop-tech vendor's server log showing which hedge fund just scraped the same neighborhood you underwrite. Spies today are **data feeds**, **human networks**, and **mentors** with scar tissue on every finger. Your task is to recruit them, decode them, and fold their whispers into a twelve-month intelligence cycle so tight that surprises shrink to minor wrinkles.

This chapter tells you how.

1   Re-reading Sun Tzu's Spycraft Through a Data Lens

Sun Tzu classified spies into five categories: *local*, *inward*, *converted*, *doomed*, and *surviving*. Translate the parchment:

1. **Local spies** — residents, site staff, neighborhood fixers.

2. **Inward spies** — employees of counterparties: assistants to listing brokers, junior loan officers, county clerks.

3. **Converted spies** — competitors willing to trade intel for favors: wholesalers with stale leads, contractors tired of flaky sponsors.

4. **Doomed spies** — decoys who feed misinformation to rivals: public facing pro-forma with false comps that hide your real strike zone.

5. **Surviving spies** — impartial sensors that return again and again: APIs, scrapers, dashboards, mentors.

> "Spies cannot be usefully employed without a certain intuitive sagacity."
> —ch. 13

Sagacity today means teaching algorithms what to watch and teaching humans what algorithms miss.

2 Covert Intel Source #1: Prop-Tech APIs

2.1 Why APIs Are Surviving Spies

An API (application programming interface) is a live pipe pumping structured data from somebody else's servers into your command tent. Unlike broker e-blasts—loud, slow, public—APIs whisper date-stamped factoids the moment they change.

- **Rent-roll aggregators** push anonymized lease transactions from property-management software.

- **Foot-traffic analytics** deliver mobile-device pings around target corners.

- **Construction-permit feeds** refresh every hour with new filings.

With a few hundred lines of code you own a battalion of tireless spies that cost less per month than one intern.

2.2 Top API Categories

- **Lease-Pricing Streams** – RealPage, Yardi Matrix, or smaller scrapers like RentHub. They reveal not *ask* rents but signed leases.

- **Transaction Registries** – PropStream, Reonomy, Attom. Data delivered JSON: deed transfers, mortgage liens, foreclosure filings.

- **Credit-Card Spend** – Placer.ai or SafeGraph Merchant; traffic converting into sales volumes near your retail pad.

- **Ride-Share Logs** – Some cities open Lyft/Uber API clusters: pick-up density predicts gentrification corridors sooner than MLS.

- **Climate-Risk Scores** – Jupiter or ClimateCheck APIs feed parcel-level flood/heat projections to underwrite insurance forward.

2.3 Operationalizing

1. **Define Questions First** – "Which zip codes saw ≥5 signed leases last week at rents ≥10 % above trailing median?"

2. **Write Cron Jobs** – Python script pulls at 3 a.m.; loads PostgreSQL.

3. **Trigger Alerts** – If condition met, Slack bot pings acquisitions channel with link to parcel.

4. **Archive Raw Feeds** – Six-month history turns into trendline; spies without memory forget what they learned.

> "Knowledge of the enemy's dispositions can only be obtained from other men."
> —ch. 13

APIs *are* "other men," just silicon-based.

---

3 Covert Intel Source #2: Deed-Data Scrapers

3.1 The Edge in Micro-Timing

County recorders post deeds, mortgages, lis-pendens hours—or days—before third-party vendors ingest and sell them. A headless browser pointed at clerk webpages can spot that a 96-unit deed recorded at 10:17 a.m. under a shell LLC you've never heard of. By lunch you can triangulate the lawyer, guess the buyer's cap stack, and decide whether to intercept limited partners disappointed they were sized out.

3.2 Build or Buy?

- **Open-Source Stack** – Selenium or Playwright scripts store PDFs, parse via Tesseract OCR.

- **Cloud Scraper Services** – Datascrape.io or Import.io manage proxies; you pay per thousand records.

* **Hybrid** – Build core parser; rent IP rotation so counties don't ban you.

3.3 Ethics and Legality

Public records are public. The gray line is *rate* and *intent.* Throttle requests; obey robots.txt when present. And never scrape personal identifiers beyond basics needed for underwriting.

3.4 Case Snap

A sponsor scraped Orange County clerk site hourly. Flagged 26-acre industrial tract deeded to a single-purpose entity linked to a known solar-logistics fund. Before press discovered, he optioned two adjacent five-acre parcels, flipping them three months later to the same fund at 4× premium. Data beat drones.

---

4 Covert Intel Source #3: City Planners and Bureaucrats

> "Of all the varieties of spies, none are more important than those who have served the enemy for a long period of time… These are men of infinite resource."
> —ch. 13

Planners, permit clerks, utility-field inspectors—none wear your jersey, yet they patrol trenches you never reach. They see:

- **Pre-application sketches** two years before public hearings.

- **Water-capacity studies** that telegraph future density caps.

- **Quiet moratorium memos** whispers before city council votes.

Winning their trust converts them into the highest-ROI local spies.

4.1 Cultivation Protocol

1. **Respect the Grind** – Bureaucrats feel undervalued; ask about workloads, process pain. Listen.

2. **Ask Micro, Not Macro** – "If I combined lot lines here, what detail trips plan-check?" They appreciate professionals.

3. **Return Value** – Email them corrected plat map or data they're missing; you become problem-solver.

4. **Discrete Thanks** – Gift cards can breach ethics rules; instead, publicly credit them in planning-commission testimony. Recognition equals currency.

4.2 Information Boundaries

Never press for privileged docs they cannot share. Instead ask how *you* can structure submittals to sail through; their answers reveal the same insight without overreach.

---

5 Spies by Relationship Tier

Tier 1: Inner Circle
 Mentor investors, attorney, civil engineer, PM regional director—speak weekly. Confidential, strategic intel.

Tier 2: Active Network
 Lenders, appraisers, brokers, inspectors—monthly check-ins, data swaps, coffee meetups.

Tier 3: Peripheral Sensors
 API vendors, lobbyist newsletters, neighborhood social-media admins—passive feed or quarterly sync.

Purposefully classify; Sun Tzu warned spies must be managed. Tier status dictates response cadence, reward frequency, and crisis mobilization speed.

---

6 Mentors: The Human Early-Warning Radar

"Foreknowledge cannot be elicited from ghosts and spirits, it cannot be obtained by analogy… It must be

obtained from men who know the enemy's situation."
—ch. 13

Mentors are living memory sticks. They predict pitfalls no
spreadsheet can. The deal you consider "creative" they tried in
1993 and sued over in 1995. Recruit:

- **Gray-Hair Capital Allocators** – retired REIT CIOs, bank
  special-assets chiefs.

- **Niche Specialists** – brownfield environmental lawyers,
  union labor negotiators.

- **Cross-Discipline Brains** – logistics CEOs, telecom
  infrastructure planners.

6.1   Value Exchange

Pay retainers or success fees; or barter deal exposure, advisory
equity, or speaking slots. Mentorship is commerce of wisdom;
price it fairly.

---

7   Spycraft Security: Keeping the Network Silent

Sun Tzu executed spies who leaked. You won't, but protect your
edge.

- **Need-to-Know Data Rooms** – Share underwriting only after NDA, watermark per viewer.

- **VPN and MFA** – APIs and scrapers on isolated servers; rotate keys weekly.

- **Info-Firebreaks** – Don't cross-pollinate networks: what a planning clerk shares stays away from broker dinner chat.

Loose lips kill margins.

---

8   Designing Your 12-Month Intelligence Cycle (Final Drill)

"Spies are a most important element in water,
because on them depends an army's ability to move."
—ch. 13

An intelligence cycle is a calendar of tasks, reviews, and feedback loops that ensure no spy's report rots in a forgotten inbox. Your cycle combines **collection, analysis, dissemination, and revision** across four quarters.

Month 0: War-Room Setup

- Map tier lists.

- Script API pulls.

- Draft data dictionary—every field defined.

Q1 – "Orientation"

- **Collect** lease-signing feed, deeds scraper, permit filings.

- **Analyze**: Create heat-map of rent outrunners, overlay debt maturities.

- **Disseminate**: 15-slide strategy brief to partners—where acquisition will focus.

- **Revise**: Identify missing municipal feeds; allocate budget.

Q2 – "Probe & Align"

- **Collect** real-time foot-traffic and credit-card spend near shortlisted parcels.

- **Analyze** opportunity-score algorithm: rent growth minus tax increase risk.

- **Disseminate**: Acquire target shortlist; assign reconnaissance trips.

- **Revise**: Tune weightings; kill agents feeding noise.

Q3 – "Strike & Confirm"

- **Collect** in-person intel: site staff interviews, neighborhood captains.

- **Analyze** cross-check with digital feeds.

- **Disseminate** LOIs, lender app packages.

- **Revise** feedback: update permit probability based on planner hints.

Q4 – "Audit & Evolve"

- **Collect** outcome metrics: deals closed, false-positive alerts, missed steals others grabbed.

- **Analyze** ROI per intel source.

- **Disseminate** 20-page after-action report; present at annual investor meeting.

- **Revise** budget: cut low-yield subscriptions, allocate to new scrapers or hire analyst.

During each quarter sprint, implement weekly "Intel Stand-Up"—15 minutes Friday, three questions:

1. What new signal did we capture?

2. What decision did it influence?

3. What gap still blinds us?

Document answers; iterate.

---

9 Testing the Network: Double-Blind Drill

Set a covert objective: identify *before month-end* the next five deeds larger than 50 units in your metro. Only API bots and clerk scraper get the data. Human acquisitions team must tag each purchase within 24 hours of filing. Miss one → post-mortem identifies which pipeline lagged.

This exercise trains the lattice between machine and person, proving speed from raw data to Slack alert.

---

10 Metrics: How to Know Your Spies Earn Their Keep

- **Lead Conversion Rate** — intel-originated leads / total leads; target > 30 %.

- **Time Edge** — hours between filing timestamp and your awareness; goal < 6 hours (APIs) or < 24 (human network).

- **Cost per Closing** — total intel spend / number of deals closed; benchmark must beat brokerage splits.

- **Prediction Accuracy** — share of "high probability" targets that transact within 12 months; raise algorithm thresholds until ≥ 60 %.

---

11   Ethical Perimeter: Dark Arts vs. Legal Genius

Espionage tempts Gray areas: hacking listing sites, bribing public officials, insider loan leaks. The broad guiding light:

If acquiring data requires a password you did not obtain legitimately, stop.
 If compensating a source means they breach fiduciary duty, decline.
 Edge gained through felony is not edge; it is a ticking time-bomb. Sun Tzu said spies must be treated with "the most liberal rewards," yet he also served a sovereign who could grant pardons. You cannot grant pardons—protect your freedom.

12   From Spies to Strategy: Closing the Loop

Every bullet you pull from spy intel must end in a live business process:

- **Parcel flagged by deed scraper** → enters underwriting Trello column.

- **Permit intel from planner** → updates zoning risk cell in model.

- **Mentor warns of HVAC-code change** → CapEx budgets auto-inflate.

If intel doesn't alter a cell, a calendar date, or a wire amount, it wasn't intel; it was trivia.

---

13   Conclusion: The Silent Regiment

"Spies are a most important element in war, because
on them depends an army's ability to move."
—ch. 13

Your deals will march or stall on the quality of your silent regiment. Code-level APIs shove schematics across midnight cables; courthouse scraps reveal enemies' footprints; city planners leak tomorrow's land values; mentors highlight traps invisible to unscarred eyes. Gather them, feed them, guard them, and record their lessons in a twelve-month cycle that never stops turning.

Do this and you embody Sun Tzu's final lesson: the true commander seldom needs loud swords or swaggering cavalry; his victory was laid in quiet footprints weeks earlier, behind the lines, by spies who moved unseen.

Appendices

Appendix A • Deal-Vetting Cheat Sheet

A one-page, front-and-back reference you can fold into your pocket before a site walk or seller call. Each item is written as a yes/no, pass/fail, or numerical threshold so you make the "go / no-go" decision in real time.

- **Price Reality** - Does contract price ÷ in-place NOI ≤ local trailing-12 cap-rate median?

- **Debt Fit** - Can the asset hit 1.25× DSCR at *stress-test* rate (SOFR + 300 bps)?

- **Cap-Ex Cliff** - Any single system expected to consume ≥ 35 % of reserve in first 24 months?

- **Regulatory Bombs** - Any code citation or zoning non-conformity that can't be waived or cured within 90 days?

- **Tenant Composition** - More than 20 % of GPR coming from a single payer or subsidy line?

- **Exit Optionality** - At least two plausible exits (refi, 1031, recap) that pencil inside five years?

- **Sponsor Bandwidth** - Will the asset demand > 10 % of manager's weekly hours for more than six weeks running?

If *any* answer trips "fail," the sheet tells you what
document or professional opinion you must secure before
earnest money goes hard.

Appendix B • Vacancy Cost Calculator

A back-of-napkin formula that translates every lost unit into a daily
dollar burn so you can compare vacancy risk across vastly
different property sizes and rent levels.

```pgsql
CopyEdit
Daily Vacancy Cost  =
   (Lost Gross Rent  +  Turnover Repair Budget  +
Utilities & Taxes During Down Time)
   ÷  Estimated Days Vacant
```

Quick-plug shortcuts —

- Use trailing-12 average rent, not pro-forma.

- Assume utilities at 10 % of rent for garden-style, 6 % for
  mid-rise.

- Default repair budget: $300 × (age in decades) per turn if
  you lack a bid.

Print the empty formula once; keep a Sharpie in the glove box. You can price vacancy the moment a leasing agent texts "notice to vacate."

Glossary • 50 Rapid-Fire Terms

Because cap-rates and construction draws are stressful enough—no one should lose momentum hunting jargon. Each entry = term + plain-English, ten-word max definition.

1. **Absorption**   Net new space leased in a period.

2. **ADR**   Average daily rent for hospitality assets.

3. **Amortization**   Loan principal repayment schedule.

4. **ARV**   After-repair value post-renovation appraisal.

5. **Bridge Debt**   Short-term, often floating-rate acquisition loan.

6. **BOV**   Broker opinion of value.

7. **CapEx**   Capital improvements extending asset life.

8. **Cap Rate**   NOI ÷ price; yield snapshot.

9. **Carry Back**   Seller-held financing note.

10. **Cash-on-Cash**   Annual pre-tax cash ÷ invested equity.

11. **CLTV**   Combined loan-to-value across liens.

12. **CO**   Certificate of occupancy.

13. **Cost Seg**   Accelerated depreciation via component study.

14. **Coverage Ratio**   NOI ÷ debt service.

15. **CPI**   Consumer Price Index inflation gauge.

16. **Debt Yield**   NOI ÷ loan amount.

17. **Deed-in-Lieu**   Voluntary transfer to lender.

18. **Defeasance**   Bond-basket swap releasing loan collateral.

19. **Draw**   Lender-funded tranche for construction.

20. **DST**   Delaware Statutory Trust 1031 wrapper.

21. **EGR**   Effective gross rent post-vacancy.

22. **Equity Multiple**   Total cash returned ÷ cash invested.

23. **Fannie Debt**   Agency multifamily financing program.

24. **Forward Rate-Lock**   Future fixed-rate debt commitment.

25. **GPR**   Gross potential rent at 100 % occupancy.

26. **GSI**   Gross scheduled income (rent + other).

27. **Hard Money**   Asset-based, high-rate private loan.

28. **Interest Reserve**   Pre-funded account for loan payments.

29. **LIBOR/SOFR**   Floating-rate benchmarks.

30. **LOI**   Letter of intent pre-contract.

31. **LTV**   Loan-to-value ratio.

32. **Mezzanine Debt**   Junior lien or pledge of equity.

33. **NOI**   Net operating income before debt.

34. **OM**   Offering memorandum from broker.

35. **Operating CapEx**   Big-ticket replacements (roof, HVAC).

36. **PACE Loan**   Property-assessed clean-energy financing.

37. **Perm Debt**   Long-term, stabilized mortgage.

38. **Pro-Forma**   Projected financial model.

39. **QR Code Lease**   Digital token for self-guided showings.

40. **Recourse**   Personal guarantee on debt.

41. **Refi Proceeds**   Cash pulled on refinancing.

42. **RUBS**   Ratio utility billing system.

43. **SNDA** Subordination, non-disturbance, attornment agreement.

44. **Syndication** Pooling investor capital under securities rules.

45. **Take-Out** Permanent financing replacing bridge loan.

46. **TIL** Truth-in-lending disclosure.

47. **T-12** Trailing-12-month income/expense statement.

48. **UPB** Unpaid principal balance.

49. **Vacancy Loss** Rents not collected due to empty units.

50. **Yield Maintenance** Pre-payment penalty preserving lender return.

Index

The back-of-book index is double-column, micro-type, obsessively cross-referenced. Each Sun Tzu quote, every underwriting ratio, and each tool name (e.g., "Python script," "Slack bot") maps to its first detailed mention. Use boldface for main entries, italics for sub-topics, and "f"/"ff" markers for multi-page spans (e.g., *cap-rate compression* 143 ff). That structure lets a time-pressed reader flip from "BRRRR cash-out 115" to every related caution flag without rereading eight hundred pages of war stories.

THIS IS NOT A COLLECTION

This volume is part of **Ancient Wisdom Hacks**—
an ongoing body of work focused on how strategy, power, and
failure actually function under pressure.

The books are only one layer.

What you are reading is an entry point into a larger system of
interpretation, application, and expansion.

WHAT THESE WORKS ARE DESIGNED TO DO

Most people look for answers.

These works expose patterns:

- How decisions are made before they are visible
- How systems weaken before they collapse
- How power shifts before it is recognized

This is not theory.
It is applied observation.

THE SYSTEM BEHIND THE WORK

Across all volumes and future releases, three forces remain
constant:

- **Strategy** — how outcomes are shaped before action
- **Conflict** — how people and systems break under pressure
- **Power** — how control is gained, maintained, and lost

No single book contains the full picture.
Each adds another angle.

CONTINUE BEYOND THIS VOLUME

New interpretations, applied volumes, and extended works are released continuously.

To access current and future material, visit:

www.AncientWisdomHacks.com

WHAT YOU WILL FIND

- Additional applied volumes across industries
- Expanded interpretations of foundational texts
- New releases not available through standard distribution
- Future projects extending beyond books

The system is still expanding.

FINAL POSITION

Clarity does not make outcomes easier.

It removes the illusion that they were ever simple.

Ancient Wisdom Hacks
Interpretation over repetition.
Application over theory.